Think It -> Say It -> Be It

Use Your Words to Change Your Life

Think It -> Say It -> Be It

Use Your Words to Change Your Life

Second Edition

Carolyn White PhD

Carolyn White PhD

ChakraCoach@gmail.com

www.chakracoach.me

www.CarolynWhitePhD.com

ISBN - 13:978-1720556770

ISBN - 10:1720556776

Limits of Liability and Disclaimer of Warranty

The author and publisher shall not be liable for your misuse of this material. This book is strictly for informational and educational purposes.

Warning – Disclaimer

The purpose of this book is to educate and entertain. The author and/or publisher do not guarantee that anyone following these techniques, suggestions, tips, ideas, or strategies will become successful. The author and/or publisher shall have neither liability nor responsibility to anyone with respect to any loss or damage caused, or alleged to be caused, directly or indirectly by the information contained in this book.

Dedication

To all my mentors – past, present and future:

Thank you for sharing your knowledge, wisdom, and love!

To my wonderful loving husband Gerry, who spent many hours proofreading and being my "sounding board" for ideas.

Thank you for being here for me!

To you, my dear reader, I dedicate my words to you:

Let my sense of presence flow from Mother Earth.

Let my wisdom and knowledge flow from Spirit.

Let my words flow from my Heart.

Think, Say, and Be Love!

About Carolyn White PhD

I've always had a thing for "bugs." If things "bugged" me, I searched for ways to improve and change what didn't work. To me, the status quo was not always the way to go. Sometimes, what I sought to change just didn't happen. Why? Was it me, them or "it?"

When asked by a junior high school vocational counselor what I wanted "to be," I responded, "A good person ~ I want to feel good about my life and what I do!" In retrospect, I think that answer may have been a bit too Zen for a 1960's school counselor. I believe that my comment years ago set the stage for my life's adventures.

Over the last 4 decades, I've been compelled to seek answers to my questions. This journey has led me to many discoveries - and more questions. Along the way, I found that knowledge and wisdom about the human energy system provided the most resourceful answers. I sought out mentors who were wise and pure of heart. "Know and grow" – that's been my motto. These mentors shared their knowledge about yoga, astrology, numerology, human energy systems, Auras, Chakras, meridians, toning, Sanskrit, Huna, Neuro Linguistic Programming, hypnotherapy, and color therapy. I learned both the theories and the pragmatics of the human energy system. Without tools, knowledge has no point. Without a project, tools get rusty.

I've applied all my "learnings" to my personal as well as my professional life as a writer, musician, computer systems consultant, manager, counselor, and trainer. Part of my career has been spent telling someone what to do and how to get there – successfully.

With the loving support of my husband of almost 40 years and Katie, our rescue standard poodle, I write for my websites, Chakracoach.me & CarolynWhitePhd.com, share my knowledge in seminars and presentations, and volunteer as a director for the Emoto Peace Project. To-date, I have authored ten books and counting: *Chakra Mastery: 7 Keys to Discover Your Inner Wisdom*, the *Chakra Mastery* companion series of Journals, *Color Me Healthy, Wealthy & Wise: Transform Your Life with Colors & Crystals* and *My Journal Adventures with Colors & Crystals.*

Praise for Think It-> Say It -> Be It: Use Your Words to Change Your Life

"I loved the simplicity of your book, and the way in which it is positioned for a person who knows little about the subject - the importance of communication and words and how they affect our lives in some many different ways. It alerts the readers to the consequences of communication and words in both thought and spoken word and how, with the energy of these, we create a myriad of complexities around us. The stories that you weave throughout give easy explanations of points you are making and how to take action and become aware of our deep centered habits."– Penelope Ward, Australia, author of Dig Deep and Fly High: Reclaiming Your Zest and Vitality, Loving Yourself from Inside Out!

"I so enjoyed Carolyn White's little gem of a book 'Think it, Say it, Be it'

I THINK this book will greatly enhance your life

I SAY do not delay, read it today

BE clear this book will BECOME YOU!"

–Shelley Stockwell-Nicholas, PhD

President of the International Hypnosis Federation and author of over 30 books

"This handy sized book Think It Say It Be It will help you change your way of thinking so that you can proceed with confidence into a more fruitful life. You can change your attitude by simply reading and enjoying the fun "Playercises," The book does not "talk down" to you, but instead, helps you to use your intelligence to alter your mind to live a better life of achievement. Enjoy! Five stars!" – Sandy B.

"Five Stars! Excellent guide to creating and attracting what you want in life." ~ Susan R.

Preface to the Second Edition

After giving "birth" to this, my first solely authored book 5 years ago, I realized I wanted to tweak some of the items. From reader's feedback I reaffirmed the core content serves as a valuable tool for transformation and personal growth. The sixteen basic Playercises remain true to the originals in the first edition. Now, I have included the answers to Playercise 2 in the Appendix. Additionally, I created an extended and expanded workbook —*Think It->Say It-> Be It Playercises* as a companion to further explore the Playercises.

I found I needed to expand and expound on certain other areas of the original book. In several instances I added new and updated information. Since symbols are a great way to communicate with the subconscious mind, I have included additional illustrations so you, the reader, can connect with the information on a deeper level.

Contents

Playercises

Why This Book is for YOU!

You are reading this because you want change – you are seeking practical methods to get what you want out of life and ultimately, feel good about yourself. You have read a number of self-help books and found that some of them lack action steps. You are not alone!

Perhaps you have sought personal change through positive daily affirmations. You become discouraged when said affirmations only affect a temporary reprieve from your challenges. You have repeatedly recited this group of words and phrases that declare and support your personal goals, beliefs, and stories. You hoped these statements, designed to influence your mind and actions, would bring a real shift to your life. Affirmations can be a great tool in reshaping your life and improve your circumstances – if you understand how they work.

Are you among the frustrated individuals who have been applying the "Laws of Attraction" a la The Secret to their lives? This principle suggests that if you hold a thought and intention, you will attract that into your life. If you tell the Universe what you want, the Universe will deliver it to you. What The Secret fails to mention is that the projected thought needs to be well formed and ecological. You either wind up attracting nothing or attracting something that you did not really want in your life. Your "communication" with the Universe did not work.

As you will discover, words structured to produce a desired outcome generate a well-formed thought. It is not enough to just think and say, "Today I will be OK." Additionally, your thoughts need to be congruent with your actions. Those actions require an "ecology" test around your intentions for the outcome: 1) is my outcome beneficial to me? 2) Is my outcome beneficial to human kind and all living creatures? 3) Is my outcome beneficial to planet Earth?

If your ecology test did not result in all "yes" answers, then step back and reconsider your outcome. We are all interrelated energetically in this Universe – that is what ecology is all about. If your outcome is good for "all," then you are in alignment with "life" and can harness the abundant power and energy of the Universe.

> *"The meaning of communication is the response you receive."*

Words have energy. You use words to communicate with others as well as converse with yourself via your thoughts. Change your thoughts to change your experience.

What is "energy?" By definition, it is "The capacity for work or vigorous activity; vigor; power; a source of usable power, such as petroleum or coal (or the Universe!)."

Energy is intangible. You know that it "exists" as you observe the "work" it does as measured by the resulting phenomena.

You see the word "energy" frequently talked about in the context of self-help, self-awareness, and spiritual teachings. Eastern philosophy refers to "chi" or "qi" as the life force energy that sustains the essence of every living creature. "Qi" is said to be everywhere in the Universe; "Qi" is omnipresent. What, then, is this "energy" and how can you harness it?

Have you ever attended a team-sporting event in a stadium - perhaps a football, baseball, or soccer game? Maybeyouhavegonetoahockeyorbasketball game in a large auditorium. The venue is almost at capacity, with the majority of the seats occupied by loyal hometown fans. You notice that the local fans are waving flags, banners, and towels. They are cheering and clapping and you hear lots of noise.

Your nose tells you that these fans are consuming the limited stadium menu of popcorn, hot dogs, pretzels, beer, etc. You are experiencing "something" - a palpable "energy" almost like electricity in the air. All of these elements combine to create an energy form called "home field advantage."

Sport statistics bear witness to the "home field (or home ice/home court) advantage." Teams generally have a higher winning percentage when they play at home with the support of their fans. If a team doesn't have a loyal and supportive fan base, i.e. the team can't attract people to fill the seats, their home winning percentage decreases. There are not enough bodies to create that powerful "home field advantage" energy form.

Energy appears in many forms; there are many ways to produce it. Here is a fun way to create a little energy of your own: Close your eyes and briskly rub your hands together for the count of sixty. Rub them back and forth, around and around. Now, stop rubbing and slowly move your hands apart, first separating the palms and then the fingers. What do you experience? What do you notice? Without touching, move your hands farther apart and then closer together. Pretend you have a ball between your hands. Yes, you have "created" an energy ball. Play with this ball. Toss it around. When you are finished playing, place your hands on your skin. What do you notice - heat, tingling, vibration, all of the aforementioned or none of the above? There is no right or wrong – it's all about what you experience!

Energy is neutral; how you use energy, as you will discover as you read on, is what attracts experience. If you want to attract a specific energy into your life, you have to maintain that level of energy 24/7. Affirmations, stated only several times during the day are a start. What you say and think with your words the rest of the day can either carry the affirmed energy through to its natural fruition or negate your "affirming" words.

Why? Words have power and take on an energetic form when grouped together. Groups of words – communication – act like packets of energy. If you are aware of what sort of energy packets you are shooting at others in conversations as well as your self-talk/thoughts, then you will have an expectation of what experiences you will attract.

The Law of Attraction presupposes that likes attract likes. Thoughts, feelings, and actions that you project are what you receive. The Law of Attraction works if you are aware of how to ask the Universe, i.e. what "energy packets" to employ, for what you want out of life.

To be successful, Affirmations, as well as the Law of Attraction, must be supported by ALL the words you speak and think, every day in every way. It is easy and fun to learn how to make those packets of words work for you. I have even provided some "Playercises" to hone your energetic word skills while having some fun.

You need actions to create change. Remember, every action will cause a reaction. "Don't make excuses – make change!"

> *"Be careful of your thoughts; they may become words at any moment." ~Ira Gassen*

Do You Mind?

How can words be used to change your life? Wonder exactly what you are changing?

Your Mind!

The mind is a complex maze of cognitive processes that enables consciousness, perception, thinking, learning, reasoning, and judgment. The mind is intangible. Throughout history, philosophers, pundits, and scientists have offered their various takes on what the mind is and where it is located. Ancient wisdom honored a body/mind/spirit connection. Nineteenth century medical science dismissed spirit and compartmentalized the body from the mind. Contemporary quantum physics suggests that the universe – and all aspects of it, including us human beings – is holographic.

The holographic nature of the mind and body presupposes that, as every part of a hologram contains the image of the whole, every part of the body also contains the image of the whole. The Chinese ear acupuncture system illustrates this principle. In this system, there is a "little person" superimposed inside the ear. For each area in the ear, there is a corresponding point that relates to a part of the body. If this ear holograph, as represented by the acupuncture points, relates to the brain holograph, which connects to the whole body, then affecting one point of the ear will also influence the corresponding area of the body.

If all parts of your body are physically interconnected, what about your thoughts and emotions? Do you notice changes in your breathing and heart rate when you are angry? When you think about a loved one, does it bring a smile to your face?

You are really a super bio-computer, run by your "mind." This challenging task requires a division of duties just like your computer. To better understand how your "mind" works, imagine a working model with two separate functions: The subconscious mind and the conscious mind.

Modern perceptions include both the conscious and subconscious mind. This was largely due to the efforts of Milton Erickson, M.D. (1901-1980), who brought to light the functioning of both the conscious and subconscious minds. Dr. Erickson assisted his patients transform their lives by interacting with their subconscious mind. He remarked that patients came to see him simply because they were unable to communicate with their subconscious mind.

Most of us are aware of the conscious mind; however, you are probably not aware of the subconscious mind. Each mind functions separately from the other. Each mind is not aware of what the "other" is doing unless you access a certain state of consciousness. "Brain Wave" activity measures these "states of consciousness".

Your brain is made of billions of brain cells called neurons that use electricity to communicate with each other. The combination of millions of neurons sending signals at once produces an enormous amount of electrical activity in the brain. This activity is detected using sensitive medical equipment, such as an electroencephalogram (EEG) that measures electricity levels over areas of the scalp. The combination of electrical activity of the brain is commonly called a Brain Wave pattern because of its cyclic, 'wave-like' nature. Your mind regulates its activities by means of electric waves registered in the brain, emitting tiny electrochemical impulses of varied frequencies that the EEG quantifies. Scientists have determined that a certain range of brainwave frequencies is associated with specific types of activities and states of consciousness. These brainwave states are:

1. Delta - .01 to 4 Hz. (Hz=Hertz, i.e. a frequency of 13 to 60 pulses, or cycles, per second). Delta brainwaves occur during deep sleep or catalepsy.

You have no awareness of your physical surroundings.

2. Theta - 4 to 7 Hz. Theta brainwaves indicate that you are in a state of somnolence with reduced awareness of your surroundings.

3. Alpha – 7 to 12 Hz. Alpha brainwaves occur when you are in a state of physical and mental relaxation. You continue to be aware of what is happening around you.

4. Beta – 12 to 30 Hz. Beta brainwaves are recorded when you are consciously alert, or you feel agitated, tense, or afraid. This is the state with the most brain wave activity.

5. Gamma – 30 to 100+ Hz. Gamma is associated with peak performance, extreme focus, and forming and retrieving memories. World class athletes, meditating monks and healers often exhibit this gamma range of brain waves.

When I originally studied brain wave frequencies 30+ years ago, Beta was considered the fastest brain wave, ranging from 13 Hz to 60 Hz. Recent research has refined these ranges, adding the gamma range. One theory suggests gamma brain waves may play a role in creating the unity of conscious perception and is involved with actualizing self-awareness.

Your waking hours are generally spent generating beta brain waves. Through extensive research, neuroscientists have demonstrated if you reduce

Human Brain Wave Frequencies

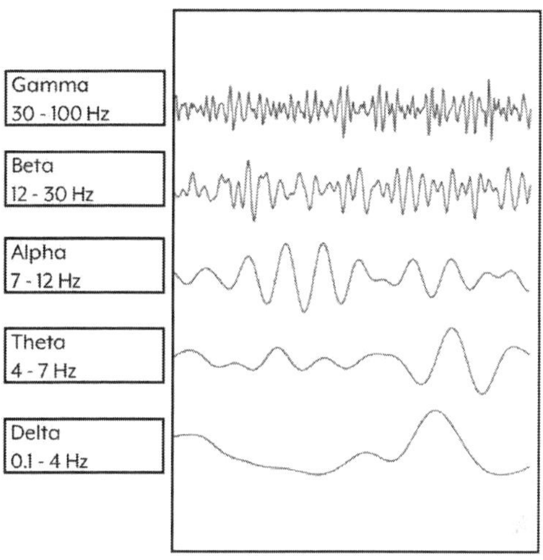

your brain waves to alpha, you achieve the ideal conditions to learn and retain new information, perform elaborate tasks, and analyze complex situations. It is also an ideal state for synthetic thought and creativity. The studies, which analyzed EEG's of test subjects, showed that the attainment of the alpha state, via attentive relaxation, produced significant increases in the levels of brain chemicals beta-endorphin, norepinephrine and dopamine. These specific brain chemicals are linked to feelings of expanded mental clarity and the formation of memories. This effect lasts for hours and even days.

According to research, the alpha state enhances the brain functions of the right hemisphere of the brain, such as the ability to create images, visualize, make associations and deal with emotions. Alpha brainwaves are a resourceful state for learning, forming new memories, and communicating between your conscious and subconscious minds. Your words are more effective for creating change when your brainwaves are in alpha mode.

Mother Earth and Your Brain Waves

The Schumann Resonance is the frequency of Earth's electromagnetic field. Apparently, since life began, the Earth has been radiating this natural frequency pulsation of 7.83 Hz. It is believed this is what the ancient Indian Rishis call "AUM," the sound of creation.

Our planet's resonant frequency has risen from a fairly steady 7.8 Hz in the late 1980's to 13 Hz in 2016. For years, this frequency hovered around 7.8 Hz with only slight variations. In November 2014, a spike to 24 Hz occurred. Since then numerous spikes have happened. On January 31, 2017, this frequency peaked at 36 Hz.

The Schumann frequency at 7.83 Hz. is said to be in tune with our brain's alpha & theta brainwaves – the dream state. When stimulated, this frequency is associated with relaxation, meditation, and increased human growth hormone levels along with cerebral blood flow.

A range from 8 to 16.5 Hz takes us from the dreamy theta to the full alpha state with more alert beta frequencies starting to appear. Sudden spikes between 12-18.5 Hz result in an awakened calm state. As Gaia's frequency is changing, so are we. We are awakening and the effects may at first be somewhat disturbing. Collectively, we are being jolted from our optimum dream state of 7.8 Hz.

How does this recent shift in the Schumann frequency impact you? For one, you might see more people agitated and acting in an extreme manner. Perhaps you might feel apprehensive or perturbed for no apparent reason. This is why it is important to learn how to regulate your brain waves so you can access the resourceful alpha state at your command.

Remember, meditation, relaxation exercises, and activities that enable the sense of calmness support the alpha state. You will learn several breathing exercises that help you access the alpha state. Just closing your eyes and keeping them closed is one of the easiest ways to "go into alpha." When you close your eyes while awake, you remove 80% of your normal sensory input and your brain waves correspondingly slow down their rate of activity.

Let us examine the functions of the Conscious and Subconscious minds.

The Conscious Mind is the logical part of you. It is where all of your current thoughts reside and is what you refer to as "I." The conscious mind is both the input device and the programmer. It is like the "bus driver" as it has the choice, the free will, of telling you where to go and how to get there. Creative thought and inspiration arise out of the conscious mind.

Here are nine major functions of the Conscious Mind:

1. The Conscious Mind is the domain of the ego – the "I"
2. The Conscious Mind is logical and analytical
3. The Conscious Mind makes all logical decisions
4. The Conscious Mind is your will power
5. The Conscious Mind initiates ideas and thoughts
6. The Conscious Mind is a guiding parental authority
7. The Conscious Mind exists in the present
8. The Conscious Mind holds current thoughts
9. The Conscious Mind controls the mental body

If the Conscious mind is the driver, the Subconscious mind is the "bus" as it runs the body. The Subconscious Mind processes all of your autonomic functions. It also functions as a recording device since all of your memories as well as their associated emotions are stored here.

There are eighteen directives that are critical functions of the Subconscious Mind. It:

1. Runs the body and it has a blueprint of what the body is like now.

2. Stores your memories that are temporal and non-chronological.

3. Organizes your perceptions, such as regular and telepathic perceptions, and transmits these to the conscious mind.

4. Organizes your memories and is in charge of recall of all information.

5. Represses memories containing unresolved negative emotions and it keeps these emotions repressed for protection.

6. Presents repressed memories for resolution and emotional release when a significant emotion or thought is re-experienced.

7. The Subconscious Mind is the "Domain of the Emotions" i.e., the "Body Mind." (All memories have a specific reference experience. A memory with a significant emotional event is assigned priority over other memories).

8. The Subconscious Mind does not process negatives - so, say it the way you want it - i.e. telling your child "Do not forget your mittens" comes

out "forget your mittens" to the Subconscious Mind. If you want another person (or yourself) to remember anything, say, in a positive way, "Remember your mittens!"

9. The Subconscious Mind is highly symbolic - it responds to symbols and archetypes, which communicate with it.

10. The Subconscious Mind takes everything personally. Therefore metaphors produce results as it sees itself in everything. What the subconscious mind perceives it will project into the allegory.

11. The Subconscious Mind responds with instinct and habit.

12. The Subconscious Mind needs repetition until a habit is installed or information is incorporated.

13. The Subconscious Mind likes clear directions and obediently follows them.

14. The Subconscious Mind generates, stores, distributes, and transmits "energy."

15. Perhaps the most important function of the Subconscious Mind is that it preserves and maintains the integrity of the body.

16. The Subconscious Mind is a highly moral being - if it thinks it needs to be punished, it will create disease (this is why it is so important to get rid of guilt!).

17. The Subconscious Mind always seeks more and more to discover - it is highly curious.

18. The Subconscious Mind takes the path of least resistance as it operates on the principle of least effort.

The above lists clarify what each aspect of your mind – the conscious and the subconscious – does to process your reality. If you understand what each aspect does best, you can assign suitable tasks. For example, the conscious mind is a guiding parental authority. Therefore, it needs to act as a trustworthy parental guide to the subconscious mind. The subconscious mind requires nurturing and loving from the conscious mind. To love and respect yourself is to honor your subconscious mind.

Unless you intervene, the conscious mind only directs the subconscious mind 5% of the time. If you could apply 100% of the conscious mind's resources to the subconscious mind, you would be able to create the life you want. Words are one way to convince the subconscious mind to do the bidding of your conscious mind.

Here is how it works: Your conscious mind decides that you want to be a great orator. You spend five minutes a day speaking the affirmation: "I am a great orator!" Out of 24 hours, that's .3% of one day. When you were five years old, you had an emotionally charged incident. At a school play, while you were reciting a monologue in front of your school and family, your costume fell apart and you stood there with your skivvies hanging out. Everyone in the audience laughed and pointed fingers, which greatly embarrassed you. You wanted to crawl into a hole. You ran from the stage crying. Speaking in front of your school became a negatively charged emotional experience.

Now, 30 years later, your new job requires public speaking. You think that the affirmation "I am a great orator!" will help you overcome this challenge. Problem is, your subconscious mind is doing its job - it stored that emotionally charged memory from five year old you. When you think about public speaking, your subconscious mind dredges up the old emotional memory, regardless if you consciously remember this disaster or not. Your subconscious mind is again just doing its job. It is presenting an unresolved repressed negative emotion. This evokes a complex biochemical reaction inside you that consequently stimulates the next thing you feel – fear of speaking in public!

All these years, your subconscious mind has been protecting you from this unresolved negative emotion. When you consciously want to do something that your subconscious mind associates with this action, i.e. public speaking, it throws up the red flag – "Danger Will Robinson - Danger!" If you do not resolve the emotional conflict that your subconscious mind has stored, it will keep playing the same stage fright tune until your conscious mind decides to take action.

How does this happen? The subconscious mind, following one of its directives, is an excellent recorder of memories. Memories imprinted with significant energy, either positive or negative, take priority over other, less "charged" memory. Strong positive or strong negative emotion creates this significant energy. Think of emotion as "E"- motion, i.e. energy in motion. Strong emotions equate to a successful recording to your subconscious memory.

When an incident pushes your "buttons," the subconscious mind, again following its directives, returns to that spot in its memory banks and replays all the emotions that it deems are associated with that memory. It is just like your computer – if you press the icon for "Facebook," you will load the "Facebook" program every time.

Since the subconscious mind likes to take the path of least resistance, the conscious mind needs to think of a strategy that will motivate the subconscious mind to change its program and adopt a new one. You know that the subconscious mind responds to instinct and habit. Repetition of the new program is necessary until the new habit installs itself and the new information is incorporated. The subconscious mind will obey your new directions if delivered in a clear and succinct manner. To be effective, these directions must be positive, as the subconscious mind does not understand negative commands.

Now that you have a better understanding of how the subconscious mind works, it is easier to appreciate why spending .3% of your day saying one affirmation does not have much of an impact on changing your life. Research shows that you have to repeat a new habit for at least 21 days to modify your subconscious programming. In addition, to implement lasting change, your words must be congruent with the outlined strategies that communicate with the subconscious mind.

> *"Until you make the subconscious conscious, it will direct your life and you will call it fate." ~ Carl Jung*

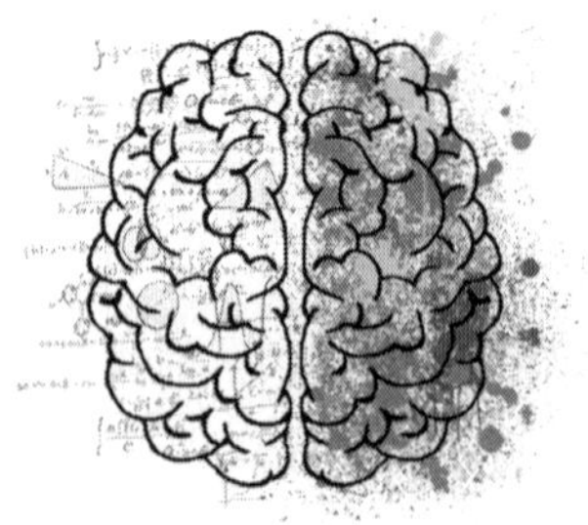

The Frequency of Change

Energy is another important aspect of communicating with the subconscious mind, as generating, storing, distributing, and transmitting "energy" is one of its directives. How can you use this "energy" to empower your words?

Energy – what is it and how is it associated with words

"Energy" – you may have an idea of what it is and how it applies to words and thoughts. You might question what type of power something as intangible as a word has over anything in this physical world. Think about electricity. It is considered a type of energy yet you cannot see it. You can see the wires that carry it along a path. You know that it exists as you experience what it does for you, from running your computer, washing your clothes, cooking your food, and lighting your house. Electricity is a form of energy you cannot really "see" - you can only "see" the results of its application.

Energy is neutral. The experiences you attract are dependent on the frequency of the energy. Just like a radio, if you want to listen to a specific station, you dial in a precise frequency. Electricity works for you when it is "tuned" to specific vibration and frequency. In North America, electricity is controlled such that its frequency is 60Hz. When electricity is regulated to 60 Hz, all your electrical appliances are happily powered. Lightning is an unregulated form of electrical energy that has the potential to destroy. In order to understand what energy can do and how to harness it, it helps to understand "Vibration" and "Frequency".

Vibration, in scientific terms, refers to a rapid oscillation of a particle, particles, or particle wave, back and forth across a central position. Frequency is the number of vibrations per second. It is measured in Hertz, which is one cycle per second.

> *"Nothing rests; everything moves; everything vibrates." - The Third Principle of Hermetic Wisdom*

The Law of Vibration is a very old concept that forms the basis for many contemporary scientific observations and theories. Everything that exists in the universe has its own natural frequency of vibration. Light, heat, magnetism, and electricity exist because of vibration. According to John W.

Keely's first law of Sympathetic Vibratory Physics, published in 1893, vibration is the beginning of all matter.

The frequency of the vibration determines its form; the lower the frequency, the more physically dense the form. A form that is more refined and subtle has a higher or faster vibratory rate. Spirit, then, vibrates at an infinite rate. If you can change the frequency of the vibration, you will alter the form.

Without frequency, which is the repetitive rate of vibration of a wavelength, your brain would have nothing to process – you would not have a basis for discriminating between the elements in your reality. Color and sound rely on certain frequencies for their uniqueness. If you slightly decrease the frequency of the color blue, it appears as the color green. If you further decrease the color blue's vibratory rate so that it is less than the visible spectrum of light, you would have infrared, which is heat. Instead of being detected by your eyes, you would now feel the effect as warmth on your skin.

The following graphic illustrates frequencies that correspond to a range of physical phenomena. The sidebar of "10s" denotes exponential factors, i.e. 10^{22} represents 10 times itself twenty-two times. Note that the Earth's frequency, as defined by the Schumann Resonance Frequency, currently averages around 10Hz, or 10 cycles per second. As previously discussed, this measurement has been increasing since autumn of 2014, with peaks spiking at 36 Hz and above.

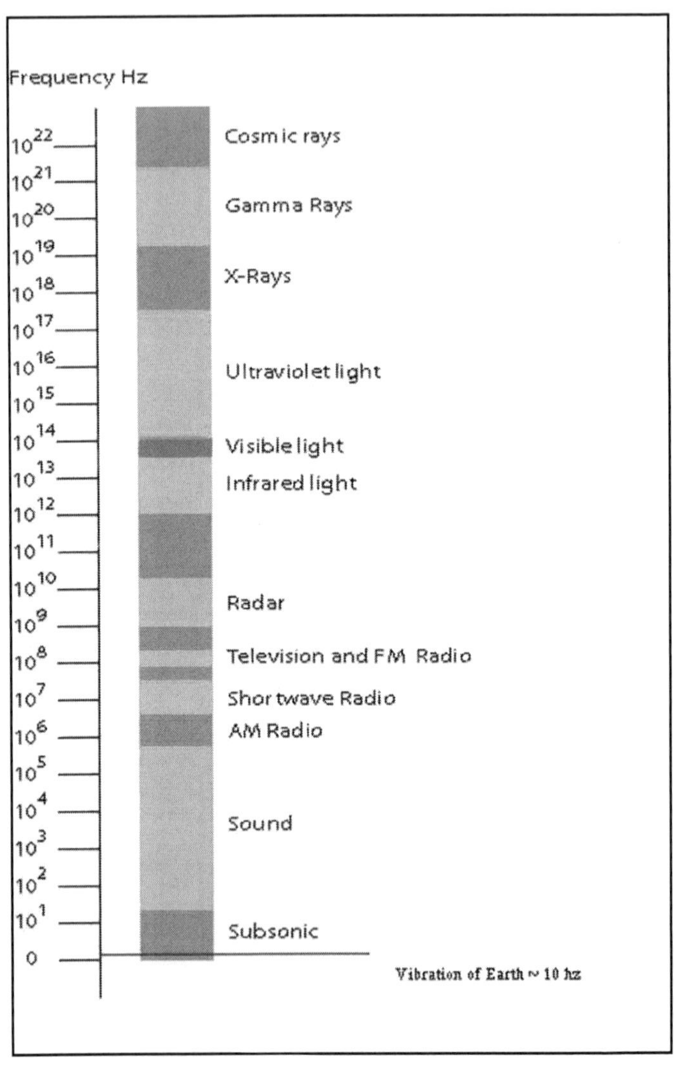

The Frequency of Energies and Corresponding Physical Phenomena

In ancient teachings, vibrations accompany all manifestation of thought, emotion, reason, will, or a mental state. Each thought, like a color or a musical note, has a corresponding frequency. If this vibratory rate is equal to or very close to the natural frequency of an object, or system, a sympathetic vibration occurs, which produces resonance. If you can consistently play a mental "tone" in the same manner as playing a pitch on a musical instrument, you can repeatedly attract the same energy. When the driving force, or the source, of a vibration matches the natural frequency of vibration of anything, resonance occurs

The field of acoustical physics demonstrates this principle. According to scientific measurements, everything in the universe has its own unique vibratory signature. If an opera singer wants to shatter a wine glass with a note, first she must tap the glass to discover its natural frequency of vibration. Then, she would sing the same note back. If she produces the correct frequency, the glass shatters when she sings the note.

When two or more electronic modules, such as clocks, are located near one another, one vibrating at a higher frequency than the other, the module with the lower frequency exhibits the tendency to match the frequency of the higher one. This physical property is called entrainment and is the premise of all energy work: If you want to transform a denser energetic form, or thought, you need to generate a frequency that is higher than this form. Through entrainment, the denser form will "rise" to match the higher vibration, changing its form in the process.

Entrainment, or matching of frequencies, manifests in many ways. Women living in the same dormitories find that their respective menstrual cycles synchronize over a period of time. If two guitars are located next to each other and the "A" string is plucked on one, the other guitar will resonate the same "A" note.

Why is it important to understand the principles of frequency, vibration, and entrainment? Here is "the secret" that *The Secret* did not mention: In order for your words to effect change, your words need to be used in a specific way and delivered with a specific energetic signature. This energy is effective in a positive and expansive way if its frequency and vibration matches levels of life promoting consciousness.

Understanding the Levels of Consciousness

Dr. David R. Hawkins, MD, PhD developed a "map" of the levels of human consciousness (also called the

Scale of Consciousness) that uses a muscle-testing technique called Applied Kinesiology (AK). Muscle testing uses your body's muscles to give a "true/false" reading. In AK, a muscle that tests strong equals a "true" reading whereas a muscle that tests weak yields a "false." AK presupposes that your body intrinsically "knows" what is beneficial for you as well as harmful. Through calibration with AK, you can figure out what is "good" and "true" for your well-being as well as what can be detrimental (false) for you.

In his doctoral dissertation, Dr. Hawkins researched and documented the nonlinear, spiritual realm. His dissertation, titled "Qualitative and Quantitative Analysis and Calibrations of the Level of Human Consciousness," is an elaborate discussion of the Scale of Consciousness and its significance. He outlines his scientifically validated work in his groundbreaking book, *Power vs. Force: The Anatomy of Consciousness* (Veritas Publishing, 1995).

Each level of consciousness (LOC) coincides with definable human behaviors and perceptions about life and God/Spirit. Each level represents a corresponding attractor field of varying strength that exists beyond the three-dimensional reality. Dr. Hawkins determined that each LOC has a critical point to which its defined field entrains.

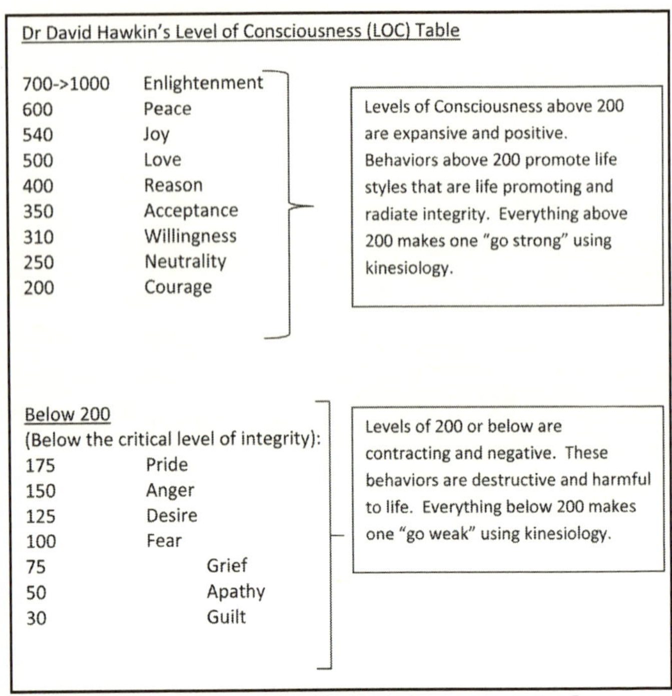

Dr David Hawkin's Level of Consciousness (LOC) Table

Level	Emotion
700->1000	Enlightenment
600	Peace
540	Joy
500	Love
400	Reason
350	Acceptance
310	Willingness
250	Neutrality
200	Courage

Levels of Consciousness above 200 are expansive and positive. Behaviors above 200 promote life styles that are life promoting and radiate integrity. Everything above 200 makes one "go strong" using kinesiology.

Below 200

(Below the critical level of integrity):

Level	Emotion
175	Pride
150	Anger
125	Desire
100	Fear
75	Grief
50	Apathy
30	Guilt

Levels of 200 or below are contracting and negative. These behaviors are destructive and harmful to life. Everything below 200 makes one "go weak" using kinesiology.

Table constructed from information in *Power vs. Force: The Anatomy of Consciousness* (Veritas Publishing, 1995)

The numbers on the scale represent calibrations of measurable vibratory frequencies of the levels of human consciousness and its corresponding level of reality. The numbers themselves are arbitrary; the significance lies in the relationship of one number, or level, to another. To arrive at this scale, Dr. Hawkins used AK on a control group. The test participants were presented with scenarios that represented each of the human behaviors as detailed in the LOC table. All participants tested weak when exposed to the behaviors listed below 200. To varying degrees, all participants tested strong to those behaviors calibrated above 200.

Dr. Hawkins points out that the two greatest spiritual growth barriers seem to be at level 200 and 500. The level of courage, level 200, represents a profound shift from destructive and harmful behavior to life-styles that are life-promoting and radiate integrity.

The second great barrier is level 500—Love. Love in this context is a way of being in the world—not a transitory emotion as most would perceive it – think of "unconditional love." According to Dr. Hawkins, the reason the level of love is so difficult to achieve is that the ego is so rooted in the physical domain as opposed to the spiritual domain, which emerges at 500.

The 400s represent the level of reason, led by the linear, mechanistic world of form. This level guided the achievements of modern society that include advancements in medicine, science, and government. Dr. Hawkins calibrated that the top echelon of intellectual geniuses, including Einstein, Freud, Newton, Aristotle, were all around 499. The 500s represent a very difficult hurdle as Dr. Hawkins determined that only four percent of the world's population calibrates in the 500s. This level denotes a shift from the linear, provable domain of classic Newtonian physics to the nonlinear, formless, spiritual realm of quantum physics.

Assume that a certain aspect of your consciousness resonates to a specific vibratory rate. This vibratory rate determines who you are and how you perceive the world around you. You have your unique vibratory rate, or pitch, just as a violin string can produce a certain pitch by placing a finger at a specific point along the string. However, many of you only play the "One Note Samba" in that you have not discovered how to change your inner vibration. The violinist can change the pitch by sliding their finger along the string, yet you may not be aware that you, too, can alter your pitch and your state of consciousness. In fact, most people do not realize how constant their pitch is.

For what purpose do you need to alter your "pitch?" At one point or another, perhaps you have noticed certain people who, when they enter a room, immediately cast a dark cloud over the people there. Even though this person may say cheerful, pleasant words to anyone present, their "pitch", their whole demeanor, exudes depression. This person's vibration is resonating to a depressed pitch; their consciousness views and reacts to the world through a depressed filter. If you want to transform yourself in any way, then learning how to change your vibration is necessary.

> *"How you vibrate is what the Universe echoes back to you in every moment" ~ Panache*

You attract energies to yourself based on your frequency and vibration. If you have regularly experienced emotions, you will attract people to you that actualize these emotions. If you think the world is a just and loving place, then you will have just and loving experiences. If you want to be loved, you first must unconditionally love and accept yourself and then radiate this unconditional love to others. If you change your words and your thoughts, you can modify your vibration.

Consider an individual who moves from financial poverty to prosperity. They have "found" the frequency and vibration of "abundance" and entrained their lives to that energy.

Sometimes, though, a person entrains to an energetic pattern that generates a cycle of pain. Abusive relationships are an example of this negative entrainment. Unless the individual in such a situation "finds" another frequency and vibration, they will continue to attract abusive relationships. This cycle of abuse is well documented - a child that is mistreated often winds up attracting a partner later in life who perpetrates this harmful behavior. Unless the abused person consciously decides to change, they will continue the cycle of abusive relationships.

> *"Surrounded by people who love life, you love it too; surrounded by people who don't, you don't." ~Mignon McLaughlin, The Second Neurotic's Notebook, 1966*

The Game Plan

Here is the game plan:

Think It: With your conscious mind, make the decision that you want to change and take your life in a specific direction. Direct your conscious mind to learn how to use your words to modify your subconscious mind's "programming."

Say It: Develop the habit of using your words. Practice, Practice, Practice! Wrap your words with positive energy and E-motion.

Be It: Live at the energy level of positive consciousness. Walk your talk! Live "as if" you attained your goal.

Playercise 1

The Four Square Breath

To begin, let us learn a Playercise that uses your breath. Breathing is one of the few automatic bodily functions that you can control with your conscious mind. To a point, you can decide how long to inhale, to hold your breath, and when to exhale. Paying attention to your breathing helps you connect to the present time.

The Four Square Breath Playercise aligns, balances, and centers your energy. This breath additionally relaxes you. It is easier to learn new things when you are relaxed. You can use this breath at anytime, anywhere, especially before your other Playercises.

The Four Square Breath is based on an ancient principle of balance between the four elements: Water, Air, Fire and Earth. Basically, you inhale through your nose to a count of four, hold your breath for a count of four, exhale for a count of four through your mouth, making a soft "HA" sound, and hold your breath for a count of four. The sequence of the breath looks like this.

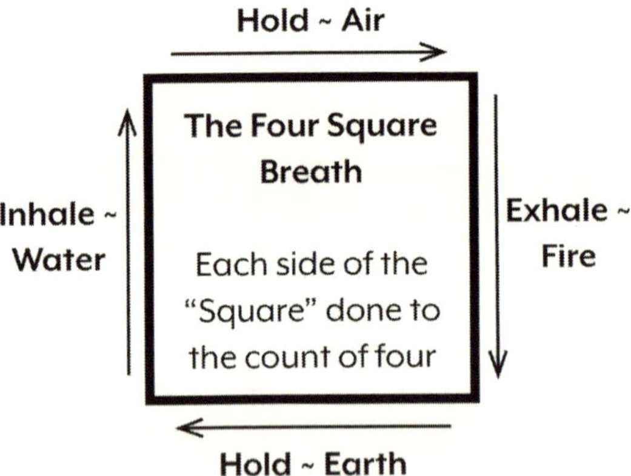

The "*Inhalation*" breath represents the energy of water as it is flowing in to your body.

The "*Hold*" of your breath after inhalation represents the element of Air. As you hold this breath, the Air element brings the energy to your head.

The "*Exhale*" breath represents the element of Fire. As you exhale through your mouth with a soft HA sound, think of a martial artist exhaling the force of their energy as they slam their hand through a board and break it. This is "Power!"

The "*Hold*" of your breath after exhalation represents the element of Earth. Earth energy is very grounding.

The first time you do the Four Square Breath Playercise repeat the "square" pattern for four cycles. Each time you do this Playercise increase the numbers of "square" repetitions.

A word about breathing for centering: The greatest benefit from breathing patterns occurs when you take a deep abdominal, or belly breath. Singers and wind instrument musicians refer to this as a diaphragmic breath as the diaphragm expands down and outward on the inhalation and pushes up on the exhalation.

Since the lungs completely fill with air, the belly expands outward. When the breath is exhaled, the belly pushes inward and up. Little babies naturally breathe in this manner as well as most people when they are lying down.

To check if you are doing this belly breath, look at yourself in a mirror, paying attention to your shoulders. Take a deep breath.

"Belly" Breathing

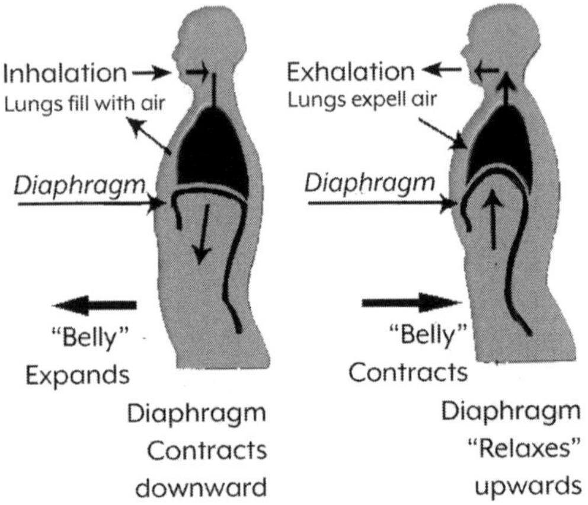

Inhalation
Lungs fill with air
Diaphragm
"Belly"
Expands
Diaphragm
Contracts
downward

Exhalation
Lungs expell air
Diaphragm
"Belly"
Contracts
Diaphragm
"Relaxes"
upwards

If your shoulders move up, you are filling your lungs only in the upper chest area. Take your hand and place it on your abdomen. If your hand moves outward with your inhalation and in with your exhalation, you are doing the belly breath!

When you breathe this deep belly breath, you are bringing more oxygen into your body. Oxygen allows your cells to radiate a steady, gentle heat. This in turn enables the body to process food and rid itself of waste products faster. Your brain is more efficient and your heart and blood stream are healthier.

The breath supports the words that you speak as they flow from your thoughts to the outside world. Maintaining a regular practice of the Four Square Breath (and other centering breathing patterns) keeps you balanced and the additional oxygen is beneficial to your health.

Conscious breathing provides many other benefits, including calming and centering your thoughts. This Four-Square breath is an excellent tool for calming the "monkey mind" arising from thrashing at too many thoughts. It is also a great way to relieve "analysis paralysis."

I teach belly breathing as a foundation in all my classes. It is the "master's" breath. Besides providing energizing oxygen to the brain and all of your cells, conscious breathing helps you to have presence in the present.

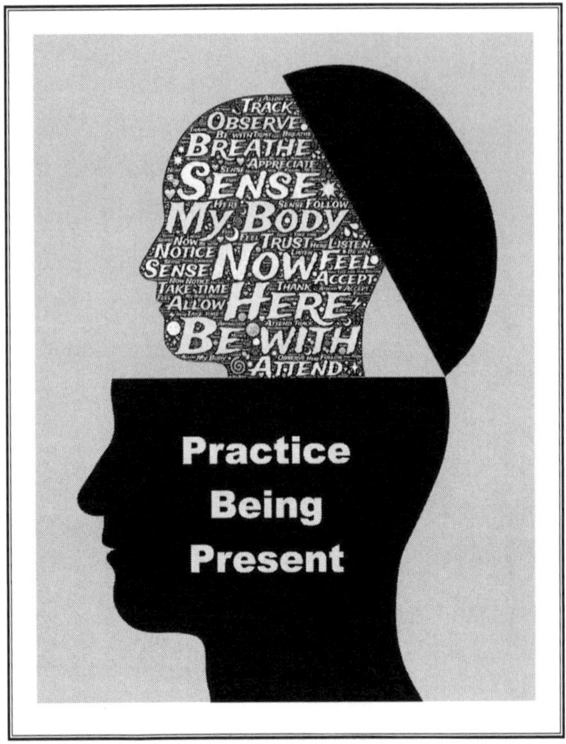
Track
Observe
Breathe
Appreciate
Sense
Sense Follow
My Body
Now
Trust
Listen
Notice
Sense
Now
Feel
Accept
Take time
Thank
Allow
Here
Be with
Attend
Practice
Being
Present

Use Your Words to Change Your Life

Politicians Do It . . .

Advertisers Do It . . .

Preachers Do It . . .

. . . use words to persuade you, to change your life!

What do you want to change? What do you want out of life?

- Vibrant Health
- A Loving Relationship
- Better sports performance
- Financial abundance
- Great Career
- ______________ (add what you want!)
- ______________
- ______________

If others use words to change your life, why don't you?

Become an exquisite communicator with yourself. Master your self-talk. Be the author of your own story – re-write your own script.

Good, now that I have your attention, let us examine how your words can change your life.

> *"The meaning of communication is the response you receive."*

Remember this phrase – write it on a sticky note, place it above your computer screen, affix it to your bathroom mirror. This phrase is your compass, the standard by which you will gauge your overall results. You are going to learn eight "word-crafting" principles that will empower you to use your words to change your life.

> *"To watch the Wonders in Alice Land" – Kennedy White, Age 3*

When our granddaughter started to speak in words common to our English language, she would often become frustrated. At these moments, she would lapse into her "own little world" language. At a loss for the right words, her communication degenerated and what she wanted to express was lost in the sniveling and babbling.

"Use your words!" her mom encouraged, "use your words so I know what you want." As soon as our granddaughter came up with a few words that related what she wanted, she went from frustration to fulfillment – her words were heard and she got what she wanted.

You use words everyday – You use words in your conversations with others - You use words in your self-talk. You hear words spoken by others. Do you really know how to use your words? Do *your words get you what you want out of life, or do they frustrate you?*

The Power of Words

"Open Sesame" opened the doors to a world of treasure for Ali Baba, as using your words can also free the riches inside of you.

"Abracadabra" casts a spell which means "it will be created with my words."

Words have long been recognized to possess power. The Devanagari, the script that represents the sounds of the ancient Sanskrit language, is referred to as the "Language of the gods." Ancient texts suggest the sound of each Sanskrit letter possesses the power of creation; the combination of these powerful sounds formats each Sanskrit word. The vibration of each word sends a resonating wave out into the universe. A form is created and an idea manifests.

The Bible reveals many examples about the power of words. The Wisdom of Solomon (18:15) tells of how "Thine all powerful word leaped from heaven down from the royal throne." In ancient Hebrew, a word, once spoken, gained a substantive existence of its own.

> *"In the Beginning was the Word, and the Word was with God, and the word was God." (John 1.1)*

> *". . . And the Word was made flesh . . ." (John 1:14)*

Words create, words manifest, and words have power! God uses words to effect change in the world. In essence, now as then, words are the instruments of creation.

Magic Words, Modern Words

Some words seem to assume a life of their own, like little packets of quantum energy, ready to unleash their magic on whoever speaks their name. Think about the following words – what do they evoke in your imagination: Abracadabra, Alakazam, Hocus-pocus, and Presto-Change-O. Do these words evoke thoughts of magic? You may not think that these words are "magical" per se, yet, if you did associate them with the conjuring of a magic spell, then they did work their "magic" on you!

Proof Positive

The late Dr. Masaru Emoto, a researcher and alternative healer from Japan, provided evidence of the magic of positive thoughts and words. The

2004 film, *What the Bleep Do We Know?* featured Dr. Emoto's seminal water molecule experiments, bringing world-wide attention to their results. These experiments demonstrated that human thoughts and intentions can alter physical reality, such as the molecular structure of water. Given that humans are comprised of at least 70% water, his discovery has far reaching implications in the realm of consciousness. Can anyone really afford to have negative thoughts or intentions?

Dr. Emoto hypothesized that water "treated" with intention can affect ice crystals formed from that water. This hypothesis was pilot tested under double-blind conditions. On November 16, 2005, a group of approximately 2,000 people in Tokyo, led by Dr. Emoto, focused positive intentions toward water samples located inside an electromagnetically shielded room at ION's laboratory in Mountain View, California. That group was unaware of similar water samples set aside in a different location as a control. Ice crystals formed from both sets of water samples were independently identified and photographed by an analyst.

The resulting images were blindly assessed for aesthetic appeal by 100 independent judges. All of the crystals from the "treated" water received higher scores for aesthetic appeal than those from the control group.

The pilot's test results were consistent with a number of previous studies undertaken by Dr. Emoto, suggesting intention may be able to influence the structure of water. In his book, *The Message from Water,* Dr. Emoto shows how water, when exposed to thoughts and words such as "Love" and "Gratitude," create beautifully formed ice crystals. Conversely, negative words such as "War" and "Hate" rarely produce well-formed ice crystals, if at all.

These experiments demonstrate consciousness has measurable effects on the geometric structure of water crystals. What does this tell us about the nature of consciousness? Is it possible that water is comprised of the same underlying "energy" as our thoughts are? Perhaps this is an incentive to give good "vibes" to our food before we eat it.

The rice experiment is another famous Emoto demonstration of the power of negative thinking and conversely, the power of positive thinking. Dr. Emoto placed portions of cooked rice into two glass containers with lids. On one container he wrote "Thank you" and on the other "You fool." He then instructed school children to say the labels on the jars out loud every day when they passed by them. After 30 days, the rice in the container lavished with positive thoughts had barely changed, while the other one developed mold.

Thoughts and words create intentions. Is this proof that consciousness and intention can affect the "physical," three-dimensional world around us? If so, then you, as a physical being, are directly impacted by your thoughts and words.

Don't let anyone else's words take away your power. No authority on earth can do that – unless you let them! Use your words to empower you!

Rapport is Representational

You are taught, in many ways, how to use language. Politicians, counselors, sales people, preachers and teachers - the most successful and persuasive individuals are taught the magic of words. Silver-tongued pundit implies a person who can weave together words that cast a magic spell over the listener, entrapping them in a net of persuasion.

The most effective communicators learned their magic though a discipline like Neuro Linguistic Programming (NLP). NLP explores the interrelationship between your thoughts, your communications, and your emotional programs. These three elements combine to generate patterns for your behavior.

Knowledge of Representational systems – how the mind processes and communicates information - is one tool in the NLP skill set. You process information through your senses of sight (visual), hearing (auditory), touch (kinesthetic), smell (olfactory) and taste (gustatory). Your five major senses, then, make up your representational systems, often referred to as sensory modalities. Since you are unique in your experiences and expression, you have your own preferred sensory modality.

When you relate your experience to others, you mentally recall what your senses associate with that experience. Then, you communicate to others with words that express your dominant representational system. If someone is communicating with you using words that match your dominant system, then it is as if that person is speaking your language.

Think about this – when you ask for directions, do you have better success finding your destination when someone draws you a map or tells you the directions? If you prefer a picture map, your lead representational system for this type of information is visual; listening to the directions indicates that "auditory" works for you.

How many times have you heard, or used, such expressions as:

"See that it gets done!"

"Sounds good to me!"

"This doesn't feel right to me"

"Something doesn't smell right to me"

"This leaves me with a bad taste in my mouth."

Each one of the above common sayings expresses a specific sensory modality. The types of words that come from your mouth describe your preferred representational system.

"See that it gets done!" – is visual.

"Sounds good to me!" – is auditory.

"This doesn't feel right to me" – is kinesthetic.

"Something doesn't smell right to me" – is olfactory.

"This leaves me with a bad taste in my mouth." – is gustatory.

The nature of the word groups that you frequently speak identifies your lead representational system.

Most of your verbal expressions use words that fall within the visual (V), auditory (A) or kinesthetic (K) sensory modalities. Olfactory and gustatory modalities apply to instincts that are more primitive. Ever wonder why successful realtors have the aroma of freshly baked chocolate chip cookies greet you at the front door of their open house? Or why there is a freshly wrapped chocolate on your hotel room pillow?

Sometimes, the words you use are more neutral, such as "think, know, seem, and understand." These are not specific to a particular modality as they hold "neutral ground" in a communication.

Perhaps you may have noticed that these identifier words are either verbs (action words) or adjectives and adverbs (descriptive words). These terms, or words, are referred to as predicates.

Why is it important to know about representational systems and your sensory modalities?

As noted, NLP studies representational systems and promotes awareness of the same because it is one way to establish rapport with another person. Rapport creates an experience of mutual trust and respect between two or more people, as if you are meeting them in their own world. When rapport exists between you and someone else, you build a bridge of friendship and mutual affinity. Communication seems to flow comfortably and intimately. You are "in tune" with the other.

Suppose your boss has frustrated you. The boss keeps telling you to "get a handle on the project." You produce flow charts, create a power point presentation, and email this to him. Boss comes back at you with "I don't feel you have a grasp of what needs to be done." By now, you are exasperated and discouraged (and maybe thinking about another job!)

This simplified example illustrates a mismatch in communication styles. Your nice flow charts and power point pages are great for a person with a visual lead representational system. Your boss's responses are more kinesthetic – i.e. he uses feeling and physical words to express his ideas. The boss is telling you that they would rather be "walked through" the information and wants you to use a more "hands on" approach. You will learn to recognize the key words – predicates – that identify each communication style.

Later, when you structure your positive self-talk, it helps to know your dominant representational system so that you can create rapport with yourself. Goal setting works more effectively when you use your dominant representational system words to change your life. You can use your words to create your own inner rapport, casting that net of persuasion over what you really want to achieve.

Rapport leads to empathy – the capacity to recognize and to understand the emotions experienced by others as well as you. When you "get" the gist of the emotional charge behind the words, you move away from judgment and towards compassion. In the English-speaking world, the word "compassion" connotes empathy and kindness for other people. In Asian languages, the word for "compassion" translates as "self-love" and "self-kindness."

Empathy and compassion begin "at home" with you. Learn what words best create rapport with your inner being. Perhaps you have been designing your goals with words that are a mismatch with your communication style. Perhaps you are using someone else's affirmations that do not resonate with the structure of your self-talk. Are you hard on yourself for falling short of your expectations? Do you judge yourself for "failing?"

> *"If you want others to be happy, practice compassion. If you want to be happy, practice compassion." - The Dalai Lama*

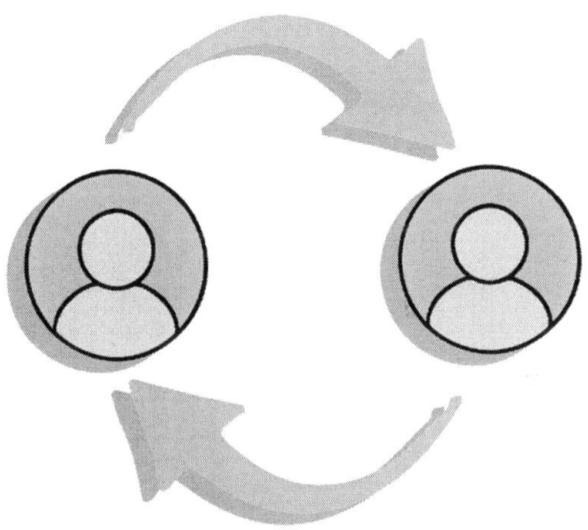

Rapport is Representational

Ready to look at, tune up, walk through, wake-up-and-smell-the-roses, and experience the sweet taste of success? Let us learn your lead representational system and create self-rapport.

Playercise 2

Sensory Modality Words

You need: Pencil or pen, sheet of 8 ½" x 11" paper

Make six columns on the top of your paper.

(The *Think It->Say It->Be It Playercise* book provides a pre-formatted worksheet.)

Label each column with the heading as follows:

Sight – Visual | **Hearing-Auditory** | **Touch-Kinesthetic** | **Smell-Olfactory** | **Taste-Gustatory** | **Neutral** |

Below is a list of words and phrases that belong to a specific representational system. Write the word in the column that best expresses its representational system.

(Answers are in the *Think It->Say It->Be It Playercise* book and the Appendix)

Clear	Handle	Feel
Catch On	Cheesy	Acrid
Picture	Grasp	Sounds Good
Tasteful	Reek	I Hear You

Focus	Firm	Illustrate
Watch	Sniff	Come to Grips
Scent	Delicious	Observe
Seem	Juicy	Viewpoint
Echo	Glimpse	Let Go
Rancid	Crunchy	Fragrance
Flavor	Stench	Perceive
Connect	Ring True	Sharp as a Tack
Visualize	Embrace	Deafening
Pungent	Infinite	Scrumptious
Bad Taste	Thud	Smells Rotten to Me

Playercise 3

Discover Your Lead Representational System.

You need: A recording device or a friend who is also reading this book. Here are several recording devices:

- Computer
- Tape recorder (getting obsolete!)
- Digital camera with movie capture
- Cellphone
- IPad, iPod
- Personal MP3 recorder
- Pencil and paper

Go to a place where you can be free of all distractions for about 15 minutes.

Speaking aloud, describe your favorite place, a pleasant experience and a favorite thing that you like to do.

If you are by yourself, record your words on your recording device. When you are finished, play back the recording. Notice the words you are using – are they primarily visual, auditory, kinesthetic? Do you say any words that are olfactory or gustatory? Are any of your words neutral?

If you are with a friend, have the friend listen to your description, noting the types of words you are using. Write down both the action words (verbs) and descriptive words (adjectives and adverbs)

If it helps, make a tally sheet, as in "Playercise 1," with columns headed V-A-K-O-G-N and make a mark when you recognize the representational system. (An example tally sheet is provided in the "Playercise Appendix section," and is available in the *Think It->Say It->Be It Playercise* workbook.) Tally up the number in each column. Your dominant representational system equals the highest word count.

You may want to repeat this exercise by describing something that you don't like to do (or a place you really didn't like). Notice if your dominant rep system is the same as when you were describing a pleasant experience.

If it is, that is OK. You are consistent and that is your uniqueness. If it is not, you have discovered an important aspect to your communications – when you like something, you shift into a different sensory modality. Being aware of this shift is valuable information; when you later develop your positive self-talk, you will use the representational system you associate with pleasant, positive experiences.

Extra credit

Want to experiment? Take different scenarios in your life and describe them - i.e. record yourself describing your work, life partner, children, home, and hobby. Note the dominant representational system used to describe each scenario. You may be surprised at the results!

Playercise 4

Developing Sensory Modality Awareness

As you go about your daily activities, practice listening for the identifier words for each representational system. Pay attention to how you respond to other peoples' words. Do you, in a conversation or while listening to a speech, experience a kinship with that person? If so, you are in rapport at that moment. Step back and observe – is that person using words that match your dominant representational system?

Become aware of the sensory words that others use. Does the speech of some put you to sleep? Is it the type of predicates that they use?

In North America, visual sensory modality seems to be the most predominant. Depending on the study, anywhere from 40% to 70% of North Americans have a visually dominant representational system.

By contrast, aboriginal folk favor the kinesthetic representational system. Remember, the predicates, or types of sensory words that you use have no relevance to intelligence–the words you use represent your internal perceptions to external events.

> *"If you were all alone in the universe with no one to talk to, no one with which to share the beauty of the stars, to laugh with, to touch, what would be your purpose in life? It is other life, it is love, which gives your life meaning. This is harmony. We must discover the joy of each other, the joy of challenge, and the joy of growth." ~Mitsugi Saotome*

According to Lynn McTaggert in in her book *The Intention Experiment*, (Harper Collins, 2008) scientific experiments have proven that co-operation is what enables life to succeed, not competition.

It is far easier to maintain a healthy, happy relationship with others that you can relate to, including yourself. Relationships start with empathy

- you cannot love anyone else unless you love yourself first.

What Part of "No" Don't You Understand?

Remember Directive #7 of the Subconscious Mind:

"The Subconscious Mind does not process negatives - so, say it the way you want it - i.e. telling your child 'Do not forget your mittens' comes out 'forget your mittens' to the Subconscious Mind. If you want another person (or yourself) to remember, say 'Remember your mittens!'"

How many times have you said to someone "Don't do (blank)" and that person goes ahead and does it anyway? Do you tell yourself not to do something and then wind up doing it? This is because the subconscious mind (and your spouse, significant other, children, friends, co-workers) does not understand what a negative means. When it hears the words "NO" or "NOT," the subconscious mind totally ignores these words and carries on implementing the commands of the word that follows.

Want proof? Don't think of a Blue Tree! OK, how many of you reading this just thought of that blue tree? Raise your hands! Now you appreciate just how the subconscious mind deals with negatives.

Often heard phrases by the subconscious mind and what it does with them:

- Don't forget = Forget
- Don't worry = Worry
- Don't' leave = Leave
- Don't smoke = Smoke
- Don't lose your wallet = Lose your wallet
- Don't dilly-dally = Dilly-dally all you want!
- Don't hurry = Hurry

When you say these words, you are subconsciously directing your actions away from what you really want. What you need to do is structure you words so that they clearly state what you want to happen. Think in terms of using your words to move towards what you want.

Instead, think of using the following words:

* Don't forget = Forget Use - **Remember!**

* Don't worry = Worry Use - **Stay calm!**

* Don't' leave = Leave Use - **Stay!**

* Don't smoke = Smoke Use - **Breathe clean air!**

* Don't lose your wallet = Lose your wallet	Use - **Pay attention to your wallet!**
* Don't dilly-dally = Dilly-dally all you want	Use - **Keep focused**!
* Don't hurry = Hurry	Use - **Take your time!**

If you want to cease a habit that no longer serves you, use words that describe clearly and positively your desired state as well as your intentions. The subconscious mind obediently responds to clear directions.

Playercise 5

Towards Do-ing

1) Pay attention when you hear the word "Don't." Listen to what others say as well as your own words. Think what word(s) are better for expressing the speaker's intentions. Use words that move toward the anticipated outcome.

2) List several things that you want to have happen in your life. Express these things with words that move towards your desired outcome.

Name the Blame Game

"Mistakes are part of the dues one pays for a full life." ~Sophia Loren

In life, you make choices. That is part of the human learning experiment. Sometimes you choose wisely, sometimes you do not. Taking what works and discarding what does not is part of learning the human lesson. When you positively reinforce what works, then you become wiser in the process and move on.

Often, though, you interrupt this learning process with the "Blame Game" – "should have, could have, and would have!" It is OK to acknowledge that something you did was less than resourceful – it is how you recognize your *faux pas* and incorporate the "learnings" for future reference.

"Should have, could have, and would have" and their negative counterparts "shouldn't have, couldn't have, wouldn't have" are phrases that announce blame. Just think, when you were a kid, how many times did you hear a person of authority, such as a teacher or parent, say, "you should have behaved better at the party – you could have taken the trash out this morning – you would have been better off not dating that person – you shouldn't have done that."

What did you experience when you heard "should have, could have, would have" – shame, guilt, regret, mischief, rebellion, defensiveness? Welcome to the Blame Game!

The Blame Game is easy to play as it does not require the instigating participant to deliver a constructive alternative or even a definitive "beef." The Blame Game tears down without building up. The slings and arrows launched by the Blame Game reduce the value of your own worth down a notch or two. Shame arises, with its emotional baggage to lower your self-worth.

You are so familiar with the Blame Game that you might play a solitaire version. These "should have, could have, would have" phrases creep into your self-talk, undermining you life's lessons. You knock down your self-worth every time that you play the Blame Game. You are also limiting your infinite self, as the results of the Blame Game are cumulative.

So, next time that you make a less than resourceful choice in life, instead of bemoaning, "If I would have left earlier, I could have made the meeting on time!"

let us play the Fame Game – Fame Game because you are the star!

"I had a choice. I chose to leave home one-half hour before the meeting. That was an interesting experience in the heavy traffic. If I want to be on time for the meeting, I need to leave an hour earlier."

When you first transition from the Blame Game to the Fame Game, it may seem like a lot more work. That is OK as, like any skill set, each time you specifically identify a choice you had and recognize a more resourceful option, the better you become at playing the game of life. Soon, once you become adept at the Fame Game, you can say to yourself, "I had a choice. I chose ______. That was an interesting experience. I learned from that. I now make different choices."

> *"Don't carry your mistakes around with you. Instead, place them under your feet and use them as stepping stones." - Anonymous*

Playercise 6

Tame the Blame Game

You need: Paper & pencil; portable recording device

During the day, each time you utter a phrase from the Blame Game, write it down or record it on your portable recording device. Note: When driving, please use a hands free recording device!

In the evening, take about 5-10 minutes reviewing today's Blame Game(s). Write one item from your list. Underneath, write down:

Tame the Blame Game

1. I had a choice. I chose __________. (Fill in the blank what your choice was)
2. That was an interesting experience. I learned ____________________. (What did you learn?)
3. I now make a different choice. Next time, I choose to ______________. (Write as many different choices you can think of)
4. Repeat for each Blame Game item.

Playercise 7

The Fame Game

You need: The results from your Tame the Blame Game, a quiet room with a mirror, such as your bathroom, and a smile.

Standing in front of your mirror, smile and read, aloud, to yourself, the responses to your Fame Game:

1. I had a choice. I chose __________.
2. That was an interesting experience. I learned ____________________.

3. I now make a different choice. Next time, I choose to ____________.

Repeat for each item. Remember to SMILE!

Good job – give yourself a pat on your back when you are finished!

Playercise 8

You Need: YOU!

Every time that you are about to engage in playing the solitary version of the Blame Game, stop and say, "I had a choice. That was an interesting experience. I now make different choices."

Smile and realize that you are making positive, constructive changes.

When you stop playing the Blame Game in Favor of the Fame Game, you also receive an extra bonus – forgiveness. Guilt and regret implant an emotional charge into any event, even the ones that seem insignificant. The Blame Game punishes; the Fame Game forgives. You realize that your choice was less than magnificent, acknowledge that and learn for future reference. Doing this implies a forgiveness of self.

> *"Forgiveness is freeing up and putting to better use the energy once consumed by holding grudges, harboring resentments, and nursing unhealed wounds. It is rediscovering the*

strengths we always had and relocating our limitless capacity to understand and accept other people and ourselves." ~Sidney and Suzanne Simon

Why is Forgiveness Important for Your Learnings?

". . . and forgive us our trespasses, as we forgive those who trespass against us . . ." How many times have those, who have grown up in the Christian tradition, recited these words from the Lord's Prayer? How often do you stop and contemplate what it really means, "to forgive" or consider the ramifications if you do not forgive. To some, these words are only words, said by rote, without any substance. To others, forgiveness is conditional on their judgment of another's or their own actions. Since forgiveness is often interwoven in religious dogma, those who have been or are alienated from the church avoid it.

What is the definition of "to forgive", the root of the word forgiveness? For starters, it is a verb, which implies action. Webster's New World Dictionary defines this verb as "to give up resentment against or the desire to punish; excuse." If you follow the meaning of "to excuse", you come up with "to release from an obligation; to permit to leave; to liberate." In Roget's Super Thesaurus, the current vernacular offers, "wipe the slate clean, let off the hook, and let bygones be bygones" as synonyms for "to forgive."

Forgiveness, then, is a process of releasing your hold on past emotions, thoughts, and deeds. If these emotions are negative and full of resentment, you are, in essence, trading pain for peace. In this process, there is an inherent catharsis - in the release, there is liberation. Samuel Clemens so appropriately summed up forgiveness as "The fragrance the violet sheds on the heel that has crushed it."

What is the importance of forgiveness - is there anything to this beyond its religious implications? For starters, modern medicine has proven that forgiveness plays an important role in your health. The Simontons', through the ground-breaking cancer research detailed in their book *Getting Well Again*,[1] have demonstrated that if you harbor resentment towards another, your stress level increases each time you recall the source of you resentment. When you recall the event, you "relive" that moment, reviving all the emotions and feelings surrounding this event. Chronic stress places an unnecessary strain on the human body, releasing excess adrenalin and placing the biochemical system in a state of imbalance.

You might direct anger or blame towards another person, perhaps feeling that the "other" is responsible for a certain wrong, i.e. a boss overlooked you for a promotion - i.e. "my boss should have promoted me!" Alternatively, you may have responded to this situation in an unsatisfactory manner – i.e. "I shouldn't have been so rude to him when he denied my promotion."

These initial incidents probably involved stress; if you do not discharge the stress and you hold onto the negative emotions associated with these past occurrences, resentment develops. Each time you replay the scenario, you experience the same stress felt during the original experience. Resentment is a "long-term re-stressing process."

As the Simontons' discovered, stress has a direct, debilitating effect on the immune system. If you do not release or forgive the past wrong, you continue to bombard your limbic system with tension and stress, further depressing your body's defenses. If the immune system is sufficiently weakened, serious illnesses, such as cancer, can develop.

It is therefore important to let go of grudges and make peace, if not directly with the other individual, at least with your memory. If you hold a negative internal representation of another then you are affecting your own internal processes and emotions. The release of guilt is in alignment with one of the prime directives of the Subconscious Mind: Since the Subconscious Mind is a highly moral being, if it thinks it needs to "be punished," it will create disease.

Therefore, a regular purging of guilt via forgiveness promotes the health of your body, mind and spirit.

> *"I grant myself forgiveness and complete absolution. For my energy has now risen above and beyond any errors I may have made in the past." – Stuart Wilde*

Often, forgiveness may appear to be a very difficult thing to do, even though it may benefit you both physically and mentally. It is easier to say that the "other" is bad rather than to clear up that part of you that feels bad. Blame, guilt, and self-hatred are all symptoms of unreleased anger towards others and one's self. Another barrier to forgiveness is the belief that what you did was so special that it is unforgivable. What you must realize is that when you forgive, you are forgiving the person, whether it is another or yourself; you are not condoning the actions involved.

> *"Forgiveness is not concerned with changing past events..."~Jack Kornfield*

When you continue to engage in resentment, it is as if you are playing tug-of-war with what was. The past holds one end of the rope and you are pulling on the other end in the present. As soon as you let go of your end of the rope, all tension disappears.

Forgiveness works in the same manner - as soon as you forgive, you immediately release all tensions,

guilt, hurt, and negativity. In essence, you have transformed the past, as forgiveness is the great release from time. When you forgive, the emotion around that part of your past disappears.

> *"Forgiveness is letting go of the hope that the past can be changed." ~ Oprah Winfrey*

When there is unwillingness to forgive, memories are kept alive that no longer exist. These memories act, then, as punishment for something that is not real. Essentially, the ego wants you to feel separate from your true self, as punishment is a form of separation and judgment.

> *"Forgiveness is choosing to love. It is the first skill of self-giving love." ~Mohandas K. Gandhi*

Future Tense

"By living in the present I acknowledge truth in my life. That strengthens me." – Stuart Wilde

English is a challenging language with words that carry multiple meanings depending on context. The word "tense", used as a verb, means, "to tighten or stiffen." As an adjective, it describes a nervous, strained, and stressful condition. In grammar, "tense" is a noun that indicates the time frame, such as past, present, or future, of a conjugated verb, as well as the continuance or completion of the verb's action or state. Remember, a verb is an "action" word.

When you want to create words of power, focus on the present, action form of the verb. Live here, be here NOW! Think of it this way, when you use your words to create images from the past, you have tightened your hold on what was – "past tense." When you couch your thought in the future, you are stressing over what you think might come – "future tense."

"If we will take care of today, God will take care of the morrow." – Mohandas K. Gandhi

Thoughts of guilt keep you living in the past. Anxiety is living in the future. Fear, which I will discuss in the next section, is a more severe form of anxiety.

"Anxiety is a thin stream of fear trickling through the mind. If encouraged, it cuts a channel into which all other thoughts are drained." ~Arthur Somers Roche

What is the advantage of using your words to live in the "Now?" If you are present in "the present," you are unaffected by memories and their emotional charge. You are free of the limitations of history, giving you more options to discover whatever comes your way. You also free yourself from the anticipation of what may come. Change takes place in the present.

"If you are depressed, you are living in the past. If you are anxious, you are living the future. If you are at peace, you are living in the present." - Lao Tzu

Playercise 9

Now is the Time!

List five to ten items that you want in your life. Remember to make these items positive and ecological, i.e. is the outcome appropriate to your values and any other outcomes you want for yourself?

Describe your life that you want "as if" it is already so. This enables the energy of your words to create your own reality.

For example:

Wear size 10 dress

Weigh 135 lbs.

Live in new house

Vacation in Maui

Work as a______ .

Share my life with my Soul Mate

Now, combine each item with "I", i.e. "I wear a size 10 dress", "I vacation in Maui."

Extra credit

Pair each item you listed with a word that matches your lead representational system and reinforces what you want.

"I see myself wearing a size 10 dress!" (visual)

"I feel the smooth touch of the fabric of my size 10 dress caressing my body. (kinesthetic)

"I hear the sales clerk say 'size 10' dress!" (auditory).

Graduate School: Make a "Manifesting My Life" Movie

Let us use several of the skills that you have learned through the "Playercises." Take one or two of the items that are on your "What I want in Life" list. Imagine a movie of the result you want. Create your movie exactly as you want and as if it is happening as you watch. If you want to weigh 135 lbs. and wear a size 10 dress, then imagine yourself entering your bathroom, stepping on the scale, and read '135' on the scale, Then, take your dress and, before donning it, notice the label that says "Size 10." Let the movie run and notice any thoughts, words, or actions that led to the results playing out in this movie.

Remember your lead representational system, the one that you most associate with the positive? Use this to enliven your "Manifesting My Life" movie. If you are visual, enhance the scene with color and "eye candy." If sound rings true for you, make it a lively talkie. If kinesthetic, get a feel for what is in the movie. If you lead with your nose, get your smell-a-vision working. Taste the essence of your ideal life – savor the flavor! The key is to create a movie your way and project your outcome in the present

If at any point your movie is not progressing the way you want, change it. It is your movie! You are the producer, director, and starring actor. Make the movie so it projects your outcome. If there are unforeseen glitches in the action, say, "Cut – I'm an intelligent director. What I did isn't unfolding as I imagined. Next 'take,' I will do it differently. I am a resourceful director and can easily change my script."

The "Manifesting My Life" movie is a great tool on several levels. For one, it serves as a "dress rehearsal" for those behaviors, attitudes and goals you want. Perhaps you discover that what you want is not ecological or you need to do "A" before you do "B." When you know that your movie works for you, multiple screenings reinforce what you want, sending out those energy waves of vibration to attract your movie script.

Mental dress rehearsals are proven, powerful tools to create an outcome. Several scientific studies have demonstrated this principle. One university divided their basketball team into three groups. The goal was to improve foul shots over an established baseline percent of completions. The first group physically practiced this foul shot on the court 30 minutes every day for 21 days. The second group made practice shots every day for 21 days as well, only they did so in their imagination, i.e. they made a "Manifesting My Life" movie. The third group did nothing.

After 21 days, the first group that physically focused on practice improved over the baseline by 60%. Remarkably, the second group – those that practiced in their mind, improved by a slightly greater margin than the first group. The third group showed no improvement & even decreased slightly over the baseline percent.

Chasing the Rabbit or Someday My Prince Will Come

> *"There are only two days of the Year where nothing can be done. One is called yesterday and the other is called tomorrow. Today is the right day to love, believe, do, and mostly live." – Dalai Lama*

Each moment of the day, use your words to state what it is that you really want. It helps if you interject emotion into these "Playercises." Make this emotion positive – give yourself a face-lift, turn up the corners of your mouth, and SMILE! When you complete your "Playercises", stand up, raise your arms above your head, smile and say "YES!"

Science has demonstrated that smiling, laughing and saying; "YES" produces endorphins in your brain that stimulate pleasure. These natural opiates give you a "feel good" high. When you feel good about something, you naturally want to repeat what you did. Each time you use your words to change your life, pack some power into the punch, smile and say "YES!"

The more you flex the corners of your mouth upward and say "YES", the more feel-good endorphins flow. In order to meet the supply, the brain creates more neural transmitters and synapses. By repeating positive physiological behavior, you are actually rewiring your brain!

Remember, you attract energies to yourself based on your frequency and vibration. If you regularly express positive emotions that are endorphin rich, you will attract people to you that actualize these emotions. Just like any self-improvement exercise, it takes practice to strengthen your energetic vibrations. Think about it–a successful house requires a good foundation. After the initial foundation is established, the framework goes up, then the roof, then the outside walls, until the house is complete.

If you are building this house, you probably have a blueprint and an expectation that you will live in it. If another person walking by the construction site looks at your house in its various stages of construction, they probably "get it" that, this is your house and you will live in it.

When you are building your life the way you want it, your friends and those who walk by may or may not "get it" that you are in the process of creation. Until you reach that point of critical mass with your energetic vibrations where you attract others that resonate with your frequency, those that don't appreciate that your "house is under construction" may challenge you.

> *"If you accept the expectations of others, especially negative ones, then you never will change the outcome." ~Michael Jordan*

You may state that you can play the piano with only one hand as you lost the use of the other hand in an accident. (One of the finest jazz pianists I have heard, Ernie Caruthers, played with only his left hand!) Someone challenges you – "That's a silly notion!" they say. In this situation, smile, thank the person, and, if for a brief minute you wanted to abandon your quest, forgive yourself. Remember that your words are law unto you. When you believe in the strength of your own reality, you create all that you want in life.

Up to now, you have learned to express three power qualities of words. Next, you will experience effective ways to create word forms, sentences, and phrases, that will power boost your words.

First, let us learn a Playercise that rejuvenates your energy. You can use this now, as well as anytime you need a super charge.

Playercise 10

Energy Zap

Remember Tarzan? With a closed fist, he thumped on his breastbone while sounding "AAAH EEEE AAAAAH EEEE AHHHHH!"

Take your closed fist and thump on your breastbone, also known as the sternum. If appropriate, while thumping, make the "AAAH EEEE AAAAAH EEEE AHHHHH!" sound. Even thumping on your sternum is effective for rejuvenating your energy.

Great! Use this technique when you require an energy boost, i.e. when driving, for the midafternoon lulls, and when reading this book! When you thump your sternum, you are activating several acupressure points that stimulate the immune system along with the thymus gland.

Kick the But Out of Your Language

No "Buts" about it!

But is a limiting conjunction

"But takes what's gone before – and throws the thought – right onto the floor." – Dr. Carolyn

"However" is "but's" snooty relative. However is a 'but' in a tuxedo!

How many times do you hear the word "but" in a conversation? How many times do you use "but" in a sentence? "But," you say, "Isn't 'but' a common conjunction?"

Yes, 'but' is one of the seven coordinating conjunctions found in the English language: "And, but, yet, or, for, no and so." "But" is a word that joins parts of a sentence together.

So, what is a sentence? Beyond the grammar syntax, a sentence is a means of communicating your thoughts in a way that is understood in your reality, as you know it. Think about kids just learning to talk

– they use one or two words and a lot of pointing (or whining!)

Essentially, when you use a conjunction, you are conjoining (marrying) two or more different ideas together in one thought. Not all of the coordinating conjunctions are happy unions!

'And' is the positive, agreeable joining of two or more ideas, such as:

"Jane mailed in her resumes and waited by the phone for a reply." In this usage, 'and' suggests that one idea is chronologically sequential to another. Each idea is relatively neutral and indicates a logical progression of events.

When you want to suggest that one idea is the result of another, you might comment, "Bob heard the tornado warning and immediately went to the basement."

If you want to suggest one perfectly valid idea is in contrast to another (frequently replaced by but in this usage): "Jane is brilliant and Sam has a good sense of humor." You are expressing two different ideas, both valid, in the same thought.

In all of the above examples, 'And' affirms that both of the ideas in your sentence, i.e. your thoughts, are positive, valid, and true. No "buts" about it!

'But' does have its place in your words. It is important to understand its energy signature in joining two or more ideas to form your thoughts. By contrast to 'And', 'But' carries a negative connotation, often denying or decrying what went before: "We had no choice but to surrender. They have done nothing but fight all night."

'But' acts like an "excuser" adding to the negativity and giving you a reason to deny your first idea: "I want to quit smoking but I don't have the willpower." You know that you need to do something and you have given yourself a great excuse why you do not really want to do it!

'But' is used to right wrongs when the second idea in your thought suggests, in an affirmative manner, what your first idea implied in a negative way: "Sally never invested foolishly, but she employed the services of a savvy investment counsel." In this sentence, or thought, your frame your first idea around what Sally did not do and you want to turn this idea around to express a contrary notion, which is what Sally actually did. "Sally never invested foolishly; on the contrary, she employed the services of a savvy investment counsel." In this case, the conjoining 'but' is used to get your butt out of a sling and say something positive about Sally.

Often, 'But' substitutes for 'That' when negativity is involved "There is no doubt but John won the match." You could say, "There is no doubt that John won the match." Using 'but' just seems to add more denial to the preceding negativity, just like you wanting to say something nice about Sally.

'But' can herald an incredulous notion, as illustrated in the following example:

"Jim lost a fortune in the stock market, but he still seems able to live quite comfortably."

Poor Jim, yes he lost a lot of cash – this is your first idea. You are amazed and skeptical that Jim is still able to exist without worry; this second idea is an unexpected contrast to your first idea. You combine these two ideas into a thought, which conveys the sentiment, "I'm surprised that Jim is still comfortable after losing so much money."

Whereas 'And' joins two or more ideas in a group, 'But' connects two ideas where one is the exception: "Everybody but Mary is auditioning for glee club." Mary is cut off, out of the picture: "With the exception of Mary, everybody is auditioning for glee club."

'But' singles out, makes exceptions, isolates, and segregates. 'And' integrates and unifies. 'But' lurks around, following negatives and doing flip-flops to cover its tracks. Its energetic signature probably arises from its Old English origins as a merging of the words for 'by' (be) and out (ut). This word evolved into butan, which in later Middle English meant 'outside, without, except and except that.'

This exceptional conjunction has been around for a long time, excluding and negating. Why, then, is it spoken so frequently in your daily words, almost subliminally sabotaging your positive flow of thoughts?

Negative suggestions are those suggestions intentionally designed to produce a state of tension, stress, anxiety, fear, or confusion, by constant bombardment. If you accept such an assault on a conscious or subconscious level, you might set up a non-resourceful conditioned reflex action.

> *"The torment of human frustration, whatever its immediate cause, is the knowledge that the self is in prison, its vital force and "mangled mind" leaking away in lonely, wasteful self-conflict. " ~ Elizabeth Drew*

Playercise 11

Kick the But Out of Your Language!

Grab a paper and pencil or pen. Turn on the TV or radio and listen to a newscast for ten minutes.

Your assignment:

Make a mark on your paper every time you hear the word 'But' spoken. Ignore the content and the context of the newscast. Just pay attention and make a mark each time 'But' is said.

After ten minutes, tally up the number of times 'But' was uttered.

Besides the probable negativity of the newscast 'But' lends its energy and augments the negative content with additional stress, tension, and confusion – all components of negative suggestions. The mass media, especially audio and visual delivery, have propagated the misuse of this conjunction to where it is in common usage.

The 'old energy' paradigm on this planet is negative, aggressive and violent; fear and guilt are used to control. From the day you were born, this control mechanism exposed you to and programmed you to accept negative suggestions as a way of life. Language and words have been perverted in order to disseminate these negative suggestions.

Now that you know certain ways that your words can work for you, it is important to be aware of HOW you are structuring your words to create thoughts, both mentally and spoken. If your words are increasing in power, just imagine the energy potential of linking them into a chain of several congruent thoughts.

Congruence happens when all aspects of self are working together for an outcome. Goals, thoughts and behavior are harmonious aligned. Putting your ideas together in this manner is like focusing a laser beam of light on your target.

Be aware of how you connect your thoughts. Energy flows where attention goes! When you walk down the street, do you take two steps forward then one back? Energetically, this is what happens when 'but' is used to associate two or more dissimilar ideas. Express your thoughts with laser like clarity.

Remember, when you are communicating with your subconscious mind, it obeys clear directions. Contrary instructions confuse it.

So, kick the 'but' out of your language! It is OK to use 'but' as a coordinating conjunction, as long as you realize how it is linking your ideas into thoughts. Be aware of 'buts' negative association as well as how it separates ideas. Use your words to change your life! Be positive, be unifying, interconnect, empower your thoughts with 'And.'

> *"In simplifying my life, I step beyond confusion. In clarity I express power." – Stuart Wilde*

Possession is 9 Points of the Law

> *"The mere possession of a vision is not the same as living it, nor can we encourage others with it if we do not, ourselves, understand and follow its truths. The pattern of the Great Spirit is over us all, but if we follow our own spirits from within, our pattern becomes clearer. For centuries, others have sought their visions. They prepare themselves, so that if the Creator desires them to know their life's purpose, then a vision would be revealed. To be blessed with visions is not enough...we must live them!" ~High Eagle*

Some things you want to possess, others you do not – to have or have not, that is the question. If you really want to possess something, then, by all means, have at it.

In English, the verb "to have" covers many bases.

Many other languages, such as Spanish, differentiate between conditional verses essential characteristics when applying the verbs "to have" and "to be."

Conditional forms of "to have" imply that what you have is, hopefully, transitory – "I have a headache," "I have lost my way." Essential characteristics are ones that are probably not going to go away easily – "I have ten fingers", "I have a PhD in psychology."

Conditional forms of "to be" also infer that what you are is temporary - "I am hungry," "I am tired." "I am a man" and "I am a woman" establish the essential attributes of one's gender that are not likely to change.

In English, you use the same verb form of "to have" and "to be" to talk about both conditional and essential characteristics. When you use your words, how do you really "know" if what you are "having" or "being" is transitory or here to stay?

What do you think when you go to the doctor and he/she tells you:

"You have cancer."

"You have a slipped disc."

"You have a broken leg."

"You have a concussion."

Do you consider that the above conditions are transitory? Do you embrace them as your characteristic? Do you perpetuate your ownership of these conditions by telling everyone, including yourself?

"I have cancer."

"I have a slipped disc."

"I have a broken leg."

"I have a concussion."

When discussing her patients' conditions, Dr. Lilia Prado, OD, my friend and a physician at Kaiser Permanente would probably tell them:

"There is cancer in your body."

"There is a slipped disc in your back."

"There is a break in your leg."

"You are experiencing the symptoms of a concussion."

Why? If a patient frames their condition in terms of an experience, then the patient does not "own" the condition. When the patient perceived this experience as transitory, the condition is less liable to cling to and "possess" the body. This attitude also puts distance between you and the condition. Do you want your struggle to become your identity?

Many years ago, Snoopy, an apricot toy poodle, was a member of our family. When it was time for Snoopy to go out in the backyard and do his business, we always knew when he deposited his "solid" matter; as soon as the "drop" occurred, he would run away lickety-split, distancing himself from what he no longer wanted to keep in his body.

If you are experiencing something that you really do not want, use your words to dissociate yourself from that condition. Saying "I have a headache" tends to lock in the condition – do you really know if you are using "to have" as a conditional verb in this case? Instead, the words "My head hurts" removes you one level from the pain. Speaking as if your head is "experiencing the difficulty" separates you from the experience. Use your words to distance yourself from what you no longer want to keep in your body!

To have or to have not . . . To be, or not to be . . . that is the question.

Let us assume that these two verbs are all about concreteness as it is easier to think in terms of absolutes as opposed to abstracts. This will also give us a power base for using "to have" and "to be." If you want a condition to be a permanent part of your life, then, by all means, use the verbs "to have" and "to be." If you want a condition to be fleeting, then use your words to describe the condition as an experience, a feeling.

"Liberty: One of Imagination's most precious possessions." ~Ambrose Bierce

Playercise 12

Possession is 9 Points of the Law.

Now is the time to write down everything that you really want to have and to be.

Every time that you want to permanently affirm an attribute and give yourself a positive, nurturing suggestion, use "to have" or "to be."

Things you will need: Two (or more) sheets of paper, pen or pencil (workbook).

1. On the first piece of paper, write, in Big Letters, "What I want to have in my life." Make each line item positive, nurturing, and ecological to yourself and others.
2. On the second piece of paper, write, in Big Letters, "What I want to be in this life." Make each line item positive, nurturing, and ecological to yourself and others.
3. After writing the lists on each page, look, one line at a time, at each item. Close your eyes, take a deep, relaxing breath, and say, "I have ______" or "I am ______."

Closing your eyes while using your words automatically puts your brain in that resourceful alpha state where your subconscious mind can best use your words to change your programming.

With ownership comes responsibility and limitations. A thought or belief you "have" about yourself limits you. Do you really want to write this "program" into your subconscious mind? If what you want will provide more resources for your life, then go for it. Is what you want "to have" ecological? Take the "Ecology Test" around your intentions for what you want "to have:"

1. Is what I want "to have" beneficial to me?
2. Is what I want "to have" beneficial to human kind and all living creatures?
3. Is what I want "to have" beneficial to planet Earth?

If you answered "Yes" to all of the above questions, raise your arms over your head and shout "YES! – YES, I know what I want to have in my life!"

> *"Treasure your relationships, not your possessions." ~Anthony J. D'Angelo*

The 'F' Word

"He who fears something gives it power over him." ~Moorish Proverb

Fear is a four-letter word.

Fear is probably the greatest block to using the power of your words. When you use the "F" word in your thoughts or conversations, it is as if a physical barrier erects around your energy. You have put your wants and wishes effectively behind bars.

What is fear? Fear is really a future projection, often with an irrational emotional charge. You are projecting that something unpleasant might happen to you and you do not know what or when. Fear is "Future Tense!" It can be "False Evidence Appearing

Real." In other words, when you experience fear, you are living in the future and ignoring the present.

> *"Love is what we are born with, fear is what we learn." – Buddhist saying*

Fear can provide a healthy warning to you in the face of danger. In the face of a growling tiger, fear can steer you to safety. Hone your discernment to recognize whether fear is keeping you from imminent danger or is rearing its head as "False Evidence Appearing Real."

> *"Don't waste life in doubts and fears; spend yourself on the work before you, well assured that the right performance of this hour's duties will be the best preparation for the hours and ages that will follow it." ~Ralph Waldo Emerson*

Using the "F" word and its close cousin, "Afraid", can disrupt your energy. I teach a class on the Human Energy System as represented by the seven major Chakras. In this class, I use a computer with a type of biosensor that displays, in real time, a representation of the Aura and the Chakras. Over the years, I have found that the emotions, influenced by thought and words, can readily alter the look of the Aura and the balance of the Chakras.

After presenting the "left-brain" information to the class, I ask for volunteers to step up to the biosensor and have the class observe their Aura and Chakras on the big screen. As a group, we view the energy field and work with the volunteer to balance their Chakras.

"Balanced" means that each Chakra is operating at an optimum energy level and all seven of the major Chakras are working together as a harmonious system. There is a better opportunity for wellness when you maintain the balance of the Chakras. This alignment of your human energy system (HES) leads to homeostasis.

In one class, my second volunteer was a woman I will call Olga. Olga was a perfect subject as she readily responded to the classes' suggestions for balancing her Chakras. Then, out of nowhere, she blurted, "I'm really afraid for my cousin!"

Instantly, the Chakras that were coming into balance went drastically "out of whack." I counseled Olga in the use of positive words and phrases. The Chakras started to improve when, again, Olga uttered several fear-based sentences. Again, the Chakras and her energy field distorted. It was a great visual demonstration on how fear disrupts the human energy field.

> *"Worry is a complete cycle of inefficient thought revolving about a pivot of fear." ~Author Unknown*

Was Olga able to balance her energy field and return to a positive headspace? I had her complete the following Playercise and, magically, her energy field and Chakras calmed down and balanced.

Playercise 13

Being Present Breath

Since you have learned that your words attract what you want out of life, this Playercise gives you a way to get into the present moment. "Playercise" this technique several times during the day. Do it for 30 seconds to a minute. Use it when the "F" word creeps into your thoughts.

1. Stop everything that you are doing.

2. Close your eyes. Closing your eyes automatically puts your brain in that resourceful alpha state where your subconscious mind can change your programming.

3. Pay attention to your breath. Notice your breath as you inhale and exhale.

4. As you take several more breaths, become aware of the air entering and leaving your body. Are you listening to your breath? Do you feel the air? Are you watching your breath move in and out of your body?

5. Continue paying attention to your breath for several more breaths.

6. Open your eyes

7. Smile

8. Raise your hands above your head and say YES!

Paying attention to your breathing helps you connect to the present time. You are aligning and centering your energy. Being in the present allows you to let go of what you do not want. Fear is worrying about Future Events Appearing Real. To overcome fear, stay in the present moment.

> *"I keep the telephone of my mind open to peace, harmony, health, love and abundance. Then, whenever doubt, anxiety or fears try to call me, they keep getting a busy signal - and soon they'll forget my number." ~Edith Armstrong*

What you fear, you draw near. What you anticipate, you initiate, create, and exaggerate. If you have issues with falling asleep and you are afraid that you cannot, your fear can create a self-fulfilling prophecy. You are focusing your energy on what you really do not want.

Fear congers up mental imagery that can physically affect you. Dr. O. Carl Simonton was a pioneer in the use of mental imagery as an adjunct to conventional cancer treatments. Dr. Simonton taught techniques that combined physical relaxation methods and creative imagery exercises. Patients were guided to use their mind to take an active part in their healing. They were taught to imagine positive outcomes for their treatment. Patients were instructed to "see" the tumor shrinking and to "picture" their immune system cells gobble up the cancer cells like the video game "Pacman."

Many of the original patients who were taught Simonton's techniques had medically incurable cancers, with an expected survival rate of twelve months. Out of 159 patients, four years later 63 were still alive; fourteen showed no evidence of any disease, while the cancer was regressing in twelve and stable in seventeen. Remarkably, the average survival rate of this group was 24.4 months, over twice the national average for similar groups of cancer patients.

From these and other results, it appears that the mind can have an effect on "incurable" cancer. The psychologist who assisted Dr. Simonton to develop the imagery exercises, Jeanne Achterberg, believes that the brain's holographic imaging capability enables this ability.

In the holographic model of the brain's functions, the reason that the brain experiences certain events as external, such as the sound of a band playing, is that it "localizes" this event when it manifests the external hologram, which you experience as reality.

Often, the brain cannot distinguish between what is external and what it believes to be "out there." This is why the remembered, or constructed, image can have as much of an effect on the senses as the "real" thing. In essence, the holographic model of the brain maintains that all experiences, whether real or imagined, are all part of the holographically organized waveforms. These organized waveforms create your perceived reality.

This explains why thinking about a frightening situation can produce the same physiological reactions as actually experiencing the "real" thing. According to Achterberg, holographically processed images influence physical function. The image, the behavior, and the physiological reactions are therefore "a unified aspect of the same phenomenon."

Consequently, belief is so important to an individual's physical health. The images you create about your physical body influence the mechanisms that regulate your body. Achterberg has observed that a patient's belief about their disease greatly influences their survivability. Interestingly, intellectually disabled and emotionally disturbed individuals who cannot relate to the "death sentence" a cancer diagnosis may represent also have a significantly lower mortality rate from cancer. Over a four-year period in Texas, these two groups only had a four per cent death rate from cancer while the state average was fifteen to eighteen per cent. Similar studies in the United States as well as other countries yielded comparable results.

In view of these findings and other evidence, Achterberg believes that it is very important for a person with any illness to muster as many "neural holograms of health" as possible. Even imagining specific immune functions can promote health. She advises you to eliminate negative thought patterns and images that may result in adverse consequences to your health.

> *"Perhaps the most important thing we can undertake toward the reduction of fear is to make it easier for people to accept themselves, to like themselves." ~ Bonaro W. Overstreet*

Essentially, fear is the absence of love. The body lives in "growth mode" when you are relaxed and happy. That roaring tiger that scared your ancestors induced the "fight or flight" response. This reaction puts most of the normal body functions on hold in order to avoid being the tiger's next meal. Once your ancestor escaped the tiger, they went back into "growth mode," relaxed and happy.

Today, many people experience fear on a regular basis. The media – TV, radio, tabloids and the internet – inundates us with words and images that evoke fear. Faced with this fear, like your ancestors, you also experience the "fight or flight" response. If you are in constant fear, the stress of "fight or flight" compromises your immune system, leaving you susceptible to diseases such as cancer, stroke, or heart disease (the Big Three maladies of modern society.)

Be aware that fear lurks around the world in many forms. Politicians use fear to sway your vote –"if you vote for my opponent, you will be up to your chin in deep do-do!" Advertisers paint fear based scenarios to motivate purchases. "Buy a burglar alarm system – your house might be robbed!" "Buy Life Insurance – you may keel over dead one day!"

Choose your motivations wisely. Are you acting because you are moving away from something you wish to avoid in your life? Are you acting because you choose to move positively towards what you really want?

> *"And as we let our own light shine, we unconsciously give other people permission to do the same. As we are liberated from our fear, our presence automatically liberates others."*
> *~Marianne Williamson*

Accentuate the Positive

"You've got to accentuate the positive,

Eliminate the negative

And Latch on to the affirmative

Don't mess with Mister In Between"

"You've got to spread joy up to the maximum

Bring gloom down to the minimum

Have faith or pandemoniums

Liable to walk upon the scene." –Johnny Mercer

Have you noticed that negativity fascinates people? Reality TV shows are more successful when they pit people against each other. Some people like to gossip about sad and unfortunate things that happen to others. News sells when slanted towards the sensational and negative. Have you ever heard a TV newscaster open their program with "Today, a thousand folks in Los Angeles committed random acts of kindness?"

When you received excellent customer service, do you smile and say "Thank you?" If you really like something you have read or watched, do you say thank you or let anyone know how much you appreciate his or her efforts? When you are dissatisfied with something, do you seek solutions to rectify the situation or do you go out of your way to loudly criticize, complain and let everyone know how unhappy you are?

Why is this? Why do some people think they are better off when they are negatively judging and criticizing than when they are acknowledging and appreciating? Do they forget that in doing so they are hurting actual human beings, who have feelings and usually have good intentions? The recipient may be doing the best they can with the resources at hand. Do the perpetrators realize that they are damaging themselves as well?

> *"Isn't it kind of silly to think that tearing someone else down builds you up?" ~ Sean Covey*

Most people are positive and find the good, but for some reason they do not say anything. Maybe they think that others will step up with appreciation, so they do not need to make the effort. If you wait for others to express gratitude, nobody will do anything, and only the negativity will be heard.

> *"Feeling gratitude and not expressing it is like wrapping a present and not giving it." ~William Arthur Ward*

The Attitude of Gratitude

Using your words in a positive manner reinforces what you want out of life. Thinking and expressing the positive generates more waves of positive energy. The more positive vibes that you send out, the more positive vibes you will attract.

Playercise 14

Accentuate the Positive

For each of the following, write as least three positive things. Read, aloud, your answers to yourself.

1. Life is good because:
2. I appreciate this in my life:
3. I acknowledge the following people for making a difference in my life:
4. I have thanked the following people for what they do:

It is all about the positive and the good.

If you draw a blank for item #4 in the above Playercise, go out and find the people listed in item #3. Give them a call, write and email, pay them a visit and thank them for being who they are or what they have done. Actions of another do not need to be life changing in order to express gratitude. If the server brings you extra napkins, smile and say "Thank You!"

Once you start into this Playercise, you might notice that this attitude of gratitude flows into your everyday life. As like energy attracts like energy, you may even notice that people are paying you complements. These could come in the form of an acknowledgment of your deeds or perhaps the way you look.

To maintain the attitude of gratitude when you receive that appreciation, simply smile and say "Thank You!"

Simply accept the complement. Why?

You hear someone tell you that they love your dress. The dress in question is old and you were going to give it away. In this circumstance, you might be tempted to say, "Oh, this old thing! I was going to throw it out."

If you did say this, you are really telling the other person that they really have no taste and you are shooting down their appreciation of you. You are making a judgment of them!

You may have just finished a musical performance that was not up to your standards. A person approaches you and relates how they appreciated your music. If you counter with, "That's the worst show I've ever done!" you are rejecting their gratitude. When you receive a sincere complement or words of appreciation, a simple uneditorialized "Thank You" keeps the attitude of gratitude alive.

"No matter how hard you try, it's impossible to be grateful and depressed." ~Robert Holden

Graduate School

Keep a "Gratitude Journal. " Every day, write at least three things for which you are grateful. If you think of more than three things, expand you list. Read, aloud, each one of these things. Do this the same time every day – make it a habit! Your subconscious mind will love you!

If you experience issues with falling asleep, then write in your gratitude journal just before going to bed. Committing your words physically on paper not only helps you to appreciate you and your life, it releases the day's tensions, helping you to have a restful sleep.

"We can complain because rose bushes have thorns, or rejoice because thorn bushes have roses." ~Abraham Lincoln

Healthy Talk

As a youngling, my mother and grandmother counseled me, "If you can't think of something kind to say to someone, don't say anything at all." Energetically, I have always felt that this was good advice. Problem was, if I applied this principle 100% to my communications, I was "tongue-tied" in delivering feedback.

Along the way, I have learned how to give positive feedback and stay "kind" by understanding the energetic potential of words. There is also a positive delivery system for feedback.

The words you use to label things create a biochemical response. Think about the sting that certain words have. Is there a feeling that you have in your body when you hear those words?

Examine words that you use and reframe them to an ecological, positive energy form.

Playercise 15

Healthy Talk

Read the following list aloud.

Notice any changes in your physiology. Which words affect you in a positive way? A neutral way?

Problem -> Challenge

Complaining -> Discerning

Selfish -> Self-Actualized

Stubborn -> Persistent

Spoiled Brat -> Loved

Idiot -> Unresourceful

Old -> Mature

Not good enough -. Perfect just as I am

Criticism -> Feedback

Never succeed-> Every Day in Every Way I Get Better and Better

Extra Credit

Add your own words to the list. Think of words that, for you, "sting" when you hear them. Think of a word that expresses this word in an ecological, positive energy form. Use the substitute word when appropriate.

Feedback Sandwich

When you go out to eat, a pleasing presentation of your food makes the dining experience more enjoyable. If the food tastes as good as it looks, you will leave the restaurant with a more positive experience and, if the opportunity arises, you will definitely return.

Constructive criticism – feedback – is more effective when served like a visit to a favorite restaurant.

Creating great feedback is all about presentation and content. You are going to make a sandwich using your exquisite word skills. Like any sandwich, you start with the first piece of bread; add the filling, which is "meat" of the comment, and then top off with another piece of bread.

The first piece of bread says something positive about that person (could also be "you" in your self-talk). This might be a positive aspect of their personality or a recent action that you appreciated. Energetically, this makes the recipient more open to what you are about to say. Get those positive vibes going!

The filling is the "meat" of the issue. Use you words to construct a description of the situation that has a neutral energetic charge. Be specific, clear, and congruent with your words.

Complete the sandwich with the finishing piece of bread. Use positive words to affirm future success and resolution to the issue. Leave the person with a positive experience.

Here are examples:

First example (what you may have said before reading this book) dealing with a co-worker:

"Bob – you are an idiot! You never log in your time. Don't forget to clock in and out."

Second example: Feedback sandwich you create with your words to elicit the positive outcome you want.

"Bob – you are a hard working team member. It's come to my attention that we are missing time punches for you. If you want your pay check to be accurate and reflect all the hours you worked, please remember to clock in and out on your shift."

Extra credit

In the second example 1) identify each part of the feedback sandwich; 2) for each part of the "sandwich," describe how that part uses words for positive reinforcement. (Answers are in the *Think It -> Say it -> Be It Playercise* workbook!)

Like any good cook, it takes practice to create delicious and nutritious sandwiches. Keep practicing – soon, your subconscious mind will be serving up great sandwich recipes! Remember, the "The meaning of communication is the response you receive."

Sometime, life happens. You take the high road in your communications, use your words wisely, and follow what you believe is the most ecological response to the situation. Yet, you do not receive the response you anticipated. You have a choice. Is it worth your time and energy to invest in getting the response you want? The other person may have an agenda of his or her own. Sometimes their agenda may be negative. Faced with a verbal assault of toxic words, consider if you really want to involve yourself in an energetic tug-of-war. Sometimes, it is best to not say anything and walk away.

> *"Among my most prized possessions are words that I have never spoken." ~Orson Rega Card*

Good Vibrations

Now you have the word tools to create your life, how can you energize others to be more positively receptive to your words?

I have spent several summers managing and training seasonal employees for the hospitality industry. After sixty days, I am required to have a review with each of my staff.

During one review, Kate asked me how to deal with customers who acted "unreasonably." I explained that what may seem unreasonable to her might be perfectly reasonable in the other person's model of their world. Kate elaborated that it seemed as if she often experienced "negative vibes" from certain people. I suggested that Kate do the following Playercise.

Playercise 16

Good Vibrations

Be proactive! When you know that you will need to interact with a stranger in a business situation or social situation do the following:

1. Look at the person with positive neutrality. Find one feature about this person that you like or find pleasing. This can be anything from a pleasing smile to an attractive pair of glasses. No matter how insignificant, discover one aspect of the individual that is positive in your world.

2. When you found that one thing, use your words to create a well-formed, positive thought about the person. "She has a friendly smile." "What a great pair of glasses!"

3. As you look at that person, think your well-formed positive thought.

4. Keep thinking that thought. Acknowledge that person with a smile.

The End . . . or the Beginning?

> *"We must always change, renew, rejuvenate ourselves, otherwise we harden." – Johann Wolfgang Von Goethe*

Congratulations! You have completed the first steps in using your words to change your life! This is not the end of the story – it is the beginning of your journey to use your words to change your life!

Along the way, you will discover more new and wonderful ideas and techniques. Radiate your energy through your thoughts, words, and deeds. Remember that what you project will echo back through your life.

Let's look at your recipe for success from what you have learned:

1. **Breathe** – yes, you do this all the time (I hope!). A calm, steady, aware breath centers you in the present moment. Refer to the Four Square Breath Playercise and the Being Present Breath Playercise.

2. **Think It** – use your words to create thoughts about what you want in life.

"Thoughts Become Things... Choose The Good Ones!" ~ Mike Dooley

3. **Say It** – talk about these thoughts, even write about these thoughts. Repetition retrains the subconscious mind to do what the conscious mind wants.

4. **Be It** – walk your talk, project your positive intentions, and radiate your energy. Like a magnet, you will attract those positive circumstances into your life.

"I understand the power of my words. I speak powerful and affirming words. My actions reflect my words. I am a beautiful and magnificent being. I love myself unconditionally."

What's next?

Keep practicing! Check out the *Think It-> Say It -> Be It Playercises* workbook.

Like any time you learn something new, there are times when you might wonder if you'll "get it." When, you might ask, will you be able to use your words easily and effortlessly?

Remember the first time that you learned to ride a bicycle? Learned to drive? At first, you probably thought about every move you made. Am I braking in time? Am I turning the corner correctly? After a period of time and with rehearsal, you were able to hop onto that bike or climb into the car's driver's seat and take off – with ease. Yes, you did have to pay attention to your surroundings. The mechanics – the techniques – of operating your transportation became automatic. It was almost as if you were on autopilot.

Learning to use you words is just like learning to ride that bike or drive that car. The more you practice, the easier it becomes. Soon, you and your words will be on autopilot. You are retraining your subconscious mind.

What happens when you want to change and friends think or your family says that – well, it is weird, strange, or they just do not understand?

> *"Never give up. And most importantly, be true to yourself. Write from your heart, in your own voice, and about what you believe in." ~ Louise Brown*

Remember, you are using your words to rewrite your story. You are stepping out of your old story and creating a new one – one that better serves what you want for your life. Like an arrow shooting at a target, hone into what you really want. All other voices are merely distractions, perhaps spouting their own agenda that takes you away from your goal. Part of your process, your journey, is learning to develop discernment. As you practice and develop, you will learn to listen to your true inner guidance.

> *"In the sky, there is no distinction of east and west; people create distinctions out of their own minds and then believe them to be true."* ~ *Buddha*

If challenged by others in your journey, invite your adversary to join in "the game." Suggest that they engage in the "Playercises." All people love to play games – why not play games that develop great life skills?

> *"Be true to the game, because the game will be true to you. If you try to shortcut the game, then the game will shortcut you. If you put forth the effort, good things will be bestowed upon you. That's truly about the game, and in some ways that's about life too."* ~ *Michael Jordan*

Remember our friend Olga, who nicely demonstrated, via the Aura and Chakra Imaging Computer system, the energetic results of using the "F" word? Over the years, using this imaging system, I have witnessed many individuals balance their Chakras and align their energy just by repeating the following words:

"I understand the power of my words. I speak powerful and affirming words. My actions reflect my words. I am a beautiful and magnificent being. I love myself unconditionally."

I remind my Aura and Chakra Imaging class students that "balance," in context of the human energy system—your Chakras— is an on-going, continual process and not a static result. Keeping harmony between your Chakras and Human Energy System (HES) involves a constant awareness of this energy exchange. Balance is the principle of action and reaction. It is attuning to the continuous changes in energy, the ebb and flow of your communications with the HES. To stay "in balance", you need to tune into the rhythm of life and to keep your mind moving, your body fluid, and your spirit soaring. Your words, wrapped in the energy of your unconditional love, propel you in a positive, harmonious direction.

"All you need is Love ~ John Lennon"

"I believe that we learn by practice. Whether it means to learn to dance by practicing dancing or to learn to live by practicing living, the principles are the same. In each, it is the performance of a dedicated precise set of acts, physical or intellectual, from which comes shape of achievement, a sense of one's being, a satisfaction of spirit. One becomes, in some area, an athlete of God. Practice means to perform, over and over again in the face of all obstacles, some act of vision, of faith, of desire. Practice is a means of inviting the perfection desired."

~Martha Graham

Appendix

Answers to Playercise 2

Sight – **V**isual Hearing-**A**uditory Touch-**K**inesthetic Smell-**O**lfactory Taste-**G**ustatory **N**eutral

Clear-V	Handle-K	Feel-K
Catch On-K	Cheesy-G	Acrid-O
Picture-V	Grasp-K	Sounds Good-A
Tasteful-G	Reek-O	I Hear You-A
Focus-V	Firm-K	Illustrate-V
Watch-V	Sniff-O	Come to Grips-K
Scent-O	Delicious-G	Observe-V
Seem-N	Juicy-G	Echo-A
Let Go-K	Glimpse-V	Viewpoint-V
Rancid-O	Crunchy-A/G	Fragrance-O
Flavor-G	Stench-O	Perceive-N
Connect-K	Ring True-A	Sharp as a Tack-K
Visualize-V	Embrace-K	Deafening-A
Pungent-O/G	Infinite-N	Bad Taste-G
Thud-A	Scrumptions-G	

Smells Rotten to Me-O

Made in the USA
Middletown, DE
12 September 2021

47833423R00083